Art of Advertising

AF528143

Published by
Lotus Press

Art of Advertising

Arun Mahapatra

LOTUS PRESS

4263/3, Ansari Road,
Darya Ganj, New Delhi-110002

LOTUS PRESS
4263/3, Ansari Road, Darya Ganj, New Delhi-110002
Ph: 32903912, 23280047, E-mail: lotus_press@sify.com

Art of Advertising
© 2009, Lotus Press
ISBN 978-81-8382-205-3

All rights reserved. No part of this publication may be reproduced, stored in a retrieval system or transmitted, in any form or by any means, mechanical, photocopying, recording or otherwise, without prior written permission of the publishers.

Published by: **Lotus Press**, New Delhi-110002
Printed at: DD Offset Printing Press, Noida

PREFACE

Advertising is a form of communication that typically attempts to persuade potential customers to purchase or to consume more of a particular brand of product or service of . While now central to the contemporary global economy and the reproduction of global production networks, it is only quite recently that advertising has been more than a marginal influence on patterns of sales and production. The formation of modern advertising was intimately bound up with the emergence of new forms of monopoly capitalism around the end of the 19th and beginning of the 20th century as one element in corporate strategies to create, organise and where possible control markets, especially for mass produced consumer goods. Mass production necessitated mass consumption, and this in turn required a certain homogenisation of consumer tastes for final products. At its limit, this involved seeking to create 'world cultural convergence', to homogenise consumer tastes and engineer a 'convergence of lifestyle, culture and behaviours among consumer segments across the world. Today, advertising has become a huge global enterprise unto itself, not just generating billions in revenues, but supporting other enterprises to gain an foothold and brand status.

The present text has been designed as a referral which seeks to inform readers of not just the various facets which comprise the art of advertising, but guide them on the essentials of thriving in the advertising industry in a work environment characterised by intense competition and struggle. The agenda of the book is to enable readers to gain an insight into how the world of advertising figures in the logistics of business expansion, and incorporates case-studies and examples which would enable them to understand the techniques and rules of advertising as they are constantly being re-defined.

It is hoped that the incisive and comprehensive content of the books serves the readers well. Any suggestons for furhter improvement are most welcome.

Editor

CONTENTS

1

INTRODUCTION TO ADVERTISING

The word advertising has its origin from a Latin word 'advertire' which means to turn to. Advertising is a paid form of communication, although some forms of advertising, such as public service announcements (PSAs), are donated space and time.

Advertising is paid non-personal communication from an identified sponsor using mass media to persuade or influence an audience. In an ideal world every manufacturer would be able to talk one-n-one with every consumer about the product or service being offered for sale. Personal selling is typically a one-on-one approach, but it is very expensive.

Although advertising delivered through interactive technology might be considered personal rather than mass communication, it is still a far cry from personal selling. Advertises can provide more customisation through interactive media such as the World Wide Web, but it is not the same as meeting with every customer individually to discuss a product or service. The key point is that interactive advertising reaches a large audience just like traditional advertising. The costs for time in broadcast media, for space in print media, and for time and space in interactive and support media are spread over the tremendous number of people that these media reach.

The following are the salient features of advertising:

— *Paid form:* An advertising message is paid for by the advertiser and this distinguishes it from publicity which is not paid, for. When an advertiser makes payment, he exercises control over its contents, form schedule, and media selection.

— *Any form:* Advertising can take several forms. It could be a sign, a symbol, and an illustration. It could be a message which is either written in words or shown on TV or aired on radio. It could be a mailer received in post it could be a handbill distributed at a "street corner". Advertising could be outdoor advertising such as posters or billboards or neon signs. Any form of presentation, which fulfils the functions of an advertisement, can be employed.

— *Non-personal*: Advertisement does not include any personal selling done on person-to-person basis or people-to-people basis. It is a substitute for a personal salesman. It uses mass media to deliver the message. Advertisement is meant for a larger 'target audience and is not directed to an individual.

— *Goods, services, ideas:* Advertising can promote a wide range of products. It can also promote services such as mobile telephony, internet and banking. Besides, this advertising is used to propagate socially relevant causes such as family welfare, fuel, economy, adult literacy etc. All of you must have seen advertisements on TV advising care and caution while bursting crackers at the time of Deepavali.

— *Identified sponsor:* An advertisement is put by an advertiser. The advertiser could be a company or corporation or society or an individual. The sponsoring organisation puts either its name or the name of the brand or both on the advertisement.

— *Information:* An advertising message informs the consumers about the features of the products and their availability.

— *Persuasion:* Advertising goes beyond information. It persuades the potential consumers about the suitability of the product.

— *Target audience:* An advertising message is meant for a specific group of people who are the potential or actual users of the product. A lipstick is meant for young college girls. A luxury car is meant for, high income business and professional people. An advertiser directs his message to a selected group called its target audience.

— *Creativity:* Advertising has to sell. But beyond that-it is also an art, which employs creativity to create an ad message. Advertising as a profession employs both creative and on creative—people. Those who write advertisements are called copywriters and work in the creative section. Those who visualise the written words are also create the message so generated is produced to be put across through different media. Production and media are the two other important departments of advertising business.

— *Advertising now is practised as a profession.* The advertising industry consists of the advertising agencies with billing running to Rs. 10,000 crores per annum. Then we have a body of advertisers, mostly manufacturers, distributors, large retailers; service institutions etc. who sustain the advertising activity. We have the media consisting of the press, broadcast media (radio, TV), outdoor publicity etc. In all these three components, there are trained professionals like the Advertising Manager, the Media Manager, the Accounts Manager, the Space Selling Manager, the Art Director etc.

— *Psychological, Social, and Economic Force:* Advertising influences our attitudes and predisposes us favourably towards certain products. It is thus a psychological force. Advertising reflects the contemporary society. It is thus a social force. Advertising attempts to influence' demand and so it is an economic force.

— *A discipline:* Advertising is studied as a discipline having a body of knowledge at journalism and mass communication schools and in business schools, and now in University's regular programmes.

The function of advertising can be vied in two basic ways:

1. *As a tools of marketing:* The advertising, in the above lines has been defined as a tool of marketing. It is used as a tool for selling the products, ideas and services of the identified sponsor i.e. advertiser, through non-personal intermediaries or media. It supplements the voice and personality of the individual salesman.

2. *Advertising as a means of communication and persuasion:* Advertising presents and promotes the ideas, goods and services of an identified advertiser. In presenting and promoting an item (ideas, goods and services), the advertiser, is engaging in a very important function of communication. It informs the prospective buyers and users about the product and the producer. It,

thus, serves as a communication link between the producer and the prospective buyers who are interested in seeking the information. Surely, advertising may be taken as the most efficient means of reaching people with product information.

A part from disseminating the information to the prospective buyers about the product and the producer, the advertising serves as a mass persuader. While creating awareness and popularity, it seeks to persuade. In fact advertising is a mass persuasion. It is a more effective widespread and less costly way of establishing contact than salesmanship. Clyde R. Miller points out that "all success in business in industrial production, in invention, in religious conversion, in education and in politics depend upon the process of persuasion'.

Persuasion is the essence of a democratic society. Every advertiser in modern times intends that all creative advertising must serve more than merely inform or entertain. It must change or reinforce an attitude or behaviour. And the consumer-the average man-should recognise the advertisers persuasive intention.

Thus advertising, in its broader sense must include only its commercial functions but at the same time, it should also convey adequately its purpose. The definition of advertising in the light of the above view, may be given as: "Advertising is controlled, identifiable information and persuasion by means of mass communication media."

ORIGIN AND GROWTH

Advertising history runs parallel to, the history of mankind. Advertising as we know it today is a phenomenon hardly sixty years old. Prior to the invention of the printing, press (1450 AD) there were town criers who sold their goods through shouting Generally, this was a method of sale in fairs and market yard. This simple method was' supplemented by shop-signs. The oldest written advertising is preserved in the British museum (3000 years old). Albums (a place for writing on the wall) and stone-tablets were the media. Placards followed these. With the fall of the Roman Empire, advertising died too. Till 1400 AD, there was not much of it.

Printing press invention (Germany, 'Gutenberg') gave a boost to writing and advertising. Handbills were first printed in 1477. Soon the newspaper came up on the scene. Towards the end of the 16th century all publications in Germany and Holland carried advertisements. Product advertised were: new pamphlets; books and treatises.

Periodical advertising on, a regular basis began in the early part of the 17th century. England had a weekly newspaper. But a form similar to newspaper of today came after 50 years. Newspapers started accepting picture advertising.

In 1650s some advertisements occasionally appeared. Coffee was offered for the first time in 1652, chocolate in 1657. Handbills are the fore-runners of the present day advertisements. They appeared on the scene in the 18th century. The first daily newspaper started publication in 1702. Patent Medicines were advertised most in all the newspapers.

In 19th century advertising marked a great expansion. In 1892, the first advertising agency sprang up in London. In 1841, in the USA the first advertising agency was started. More such agencies came in the USA. In 1875, the first modern advertising agency was set-up in Philadelphia. They offered not only space selling but also many other services to clients.

Towards the end of the 19th century, creative advertisement developed. Painting came to be used in advertising.

In the 20th century, advertisement bloomed to its full form. More emphasis was laid on advertisement copy. Art services and advertisement production became more and more important. Media selection was also considered equally important. By 1920, the agencies started planning campaigns. After the First World War, advertisement got established. MR also came up on the scene. Advertisement films also became prominent. After the Second World War, there was mass production. Advertising activity therefore increased. TV also came later in 20th century as a powerful medium of advertising.

Marketing through the Internet opened new frontiers for advertisers and contributed to the "dot-com" boom of the 1990s. Entire corporations operated solely on advertising revenue, offering everything from coupons to free Internet access. At the turn of the 21st century, a number of websites including the search engine Google, started a change in online advertising by emphasizing contextually relevant, unobtrusive ads intended to help, rather than inundate, users. This has led to a plethora of similar efforts and an increasing trend of interactive advertising.

A recent advertising innovation is "guerrilla marketing", which involve unusual approaches such as staged encounters in public places, giveaways of products such as cars that are covered with brand messages, and interactive advertising where the viewer can respond to become part of the advertising message. This reflects an increasing trend of interactive and "embedded" ads, such as via product placement, having consumers vote through text messages, and various innovations utilizing social network services such as MySpace.

TYPES OF ADVERTISING

Several categories of organisations are large users of advertising, most important among them being the manufacturing, trading and service firms, non-profit institutions and the government agencies. Advertising can also be classified according to types. The principal means of classification are:

(1) By geographical spread, such as national, regional and local,

(2) By target group, such as Consumer advertising, Industrial advertising or trade advertising,

(3) By type of impact such as:

(i) primary demand or selective demand advertising,

(ii) direct or indirect action advertising, and

(iii) institutional advertising.

It is conceptually more interesting and analytically more important to classify advertising. The basis of classification, however, can be diverse, as will be evident from below:

1. **By Geographical Spread**: On the basis of geographical spread, advertising can be classified as:

(a) *National advertising:* Some 'manufacturers may' think that their target is, the entire country. 'They select media with' a countryside base. Generally large, established firms belong to this category. Among them are Hindustan Lever, Brooke Bond, Larsen & Toubro, Escorts, Associated Cement Companies and the like.

(b) *Local advertising:* Small firms may like to restrict their business to State or regional level. Some firms first localise their marketing efforts and

once success has been achieved, they spread out to wider horizons. A classic example is Nirma washing powder, which initially was sold only in Gujarat and subsequently entered the other markets. Retail stores also undertake local advertising. The area to be covered would generally be a city or a town and media would be selected which principally relates to that area.

If we discuss about the recent years, several newspaper supplements have appeared which focus on a particular city and are of direct relevance to its inhabitants like the *Bombay Times* and *Metro*. Sometimes large firms may also go in for local advertising, e.g., when they undertake pre-testing of a product especially consumer products in selected areas before embarking promotional campaign on a national level.

(c) *Global advertising:* Multinational firms treat the world as their market. Firms such as National IBM or Sony or Ford advertise globally, e.g., in periodicals like *Times, Readers Digest*.

2. **By Target Group**: It is on the basis of target groups aimed at it can further be divided into sub category as:

(a) *Consumer advertising:* A very substantial portion of total advertising is directed to buyers of consumer products who purchase them either for their own use or for their household's. The fact that buyers of consumer items are generally very large and are widely distributed over a large geographical area enhances the importance of advertising as a marketing tool. The preponderance of such advertising can be seen by looking into at random any general print media, such as newspapers and magazines etc. These advertisements are intended to promote sale of the advertised products by appealing directly to the buyers/ consumers. Such advertising is called consumer advertising. Another name for this is brand advertising, which focuses on the development of a long-term brand identity and image. It tries to develop a distinctive brand image for a product. White Star Line in Britain developed a brand image of power, scientific wonder, and unparalleled luxury for Titanic.

(b) *Industrial advertising:* Industrial advertising on the other hand refers to those advertisements which are issued by the manufacturers/ distributors to the buyers of industrial products. This category would include machinery and equipment, industrial intermediates, parts and components, etc. Because of the unique characteristics of industrial buying decision process, the importance of industrial advertising is comparatively lower than that of consumer advertising.

(c) *Trade advertising:* Advertisements, which are directed by the manufacturers to the distribution channel members, such as wholesalers or retailers, are called trade advertising. The objective of such advertising is' to promote sales by motivating the distribution channel members to stock more or to attract new retain outlets.

(d) *Professional advertising:* There are certain products for which the consumers themselves are not responsible for the buying choice. The classic examples are pharmaceuticals where the decision is made by doctors while the consumers are the patient. Almost similar situation exists' in the field of construction where architects, civil engineers and contractors are the decision-makers. Firms operating in such market segments, therefore, have to direct their advertising to these decision-makers, who are professional people. Such advertising is called professional advertising.

3. **By Type of Impact**: On the basis of impact, advertising can' be primary advertising for generic products such as tea, coffee, paints etc. These are unbranded products. At later stages, these commodities are branded and specific brands are promoted, e.g., Brook Bond, Asian Paints. 'They are called selective advertising. Direct action advertising expects immediate response from the buyers such as soliciting orders through direct mail. Mostly advertising is indirect action advertising which makes the consumers favourably inclined towards the product so that they can later on buy these products in future. Institutional Advertising can be used 1 : 0 project a positive corporate image for the company.

Public Relations Advertising (PRA)

These days, organisations are concerned with the type of image they project they have to communicate their objectives to the general public. They also have to Intake the public understand what their activities are. Public relations, in short, try to build rapport with various constituents of public such as employees, customers, local authorities, pressure groups, vendors, custo[illegible] shareholders, government and public at large. Public relations advertising helps to maintain this relationship. Its main objective is to build a good corporate image. It deals with issues rather than products and services. PR advertising is done by both business and non-business organisations. It represents management and communicates its policies, problems and performances to the public.

PR advertising generally precedes shares issues these days to create a favourable climate for the investing public. Annual reports of the companies and the chairman's speech have the potential of being good PR advertising provided they are excellently drafted. .

Purposes of PR Advertising

1. It projects a favourable image of the company.
2. It generates goodwill for the business.
3. It maintains relationship with the trade and suppliers.
4. It bursts the myths surrounding the corporate activities.
5. It creates conducive climate for the investing public.
6. It wins the confidence of the employees.
7. It takes up social causes for promotion such as-dowry, female infanticide, cancer detection etc. .It thus renders community service. It seeks public support for certain causes.
8. It is concerned with customer service and customer relationship management

PR advertising can be put into three categories:

1. Institutional or Corporate Advertising.
2. Public Service Advertising.
3. Political Advertising.

Institutional or Corporate Advertising

The basic purpose of institutional or corporate advertising is to create a favourable public image of itself. It emphasizes its name, rather than its products and services. Institutional advertising may cover the following dimensions:

1. The institute may present its viewpoint about a national cause, say prevention of blindness and the efforts it has taken to help this cause.
2. It may list its social contributions, or may emphasize its socially oriented policies.
3. It may also stress on the mission of the organisation and, its philosophy.
4. It may speak about its R & D, plants, employee welfare schemes, market position.

The Institute can communicate through a single ad or a series of ads Institutional ads are indirect in their approach, and do not intend to sell anything. It forcefully tells how the organisation is a socially responsible institution. It also tells about the nationalistic leanings of the organisation. Many companies are faceless entities. Institutional or corporate advertising gives a face to the company.

Public Service Advertising

Public Service Advertising (PSA) is also institutional advertising, which seeks to promote important social issue. It is created to promote greater awareness of public causes. The examples of such social issues, which have been promoted, are handicapped children and their help, female foeticide, national integration, flood donation, AIDS etc. Public Service Advertising is also known by various other names such as Public Awareness Advertising, Social Service Advertising and Social Awareness (SA) Advertising.

Political Advertising

As most of the political advertising is directed to public, it comes under the category of public relations advertising. Political advertising is created either by political parties or candidates. Mostly we come across such advertising at the time of elections. Election advertising either lists the achievements of the party of candidate or propagates their ideological basis. Sometimes, they are provocative too. Such advertising may become comparative, where the weaknesses of the opposition are highlighted to show their party or candidate in favourable light.

Financial Advertising

When public limited companies' invite the general public to subscribe to the share capital of the company, it is called financial advertising. In a broader sense, it includes all advertising by financial industry such as banks, car loan companies, insurance companies, non-banking financial companies etc. It also includes image building corporate advertising prior to an issue or-otherwise.

The copy of financial ad gives highlights of the project, details of the issue, crisis rating, management's perception of the risk factors, closing date of the issue, lead manager's name and address, promoter's name and address, name of the company and its address. Apart from these routine things the investing public is motivated to invest by suitable copy matter—a slogan, a promise of returns, profile of the product etc. The media used for financial advertising are mainly the print media, especially the press and to some extent magazines. Mega-issues are promoted even on TV. Issue advertisements are also put on hoardings.

Financial advertising motivates the public to invest, educate the public on various aspects of the issue, works in favour of the brokers/underwriters, and builds a good corporate image. Financial advertising still remains prosaic. In order to be successful, it should become more imaginative and distinctive.

Directory Advertising

Another type of advertising is called directory because people refer to it to find out how to buy a product or service. The best known form of directory advertising is the Yellow Pages, although many different kinds of directories perform the same function.

Direct-Response Advertising

Direct-response advertising can use any advertising medium, including direct mail, but the message is different from that of national and retail advertising in that it tries to stimulate a sale directly. The consumer can respond by telephone or mail, and the product is delivered directly to the consumer by mail or some other carrier.

Business-to-Business Advertising

Business-to-business advertising includes messages directed at retailers, wholesalers, and distributors, as well as industrial purchasers and professionals such as lawyers and physicians. Advertisers-place most business advertising in business publications or professional journals.

Institutional Advertising

Institutional advertising is also called corporate advertising. These messages focus on establishing a corporate identity or winning the public to the organisation's point of view.

Interactive Advertising

Interactive advertising is delivered to individual consumers who have access to a computer and the Internet. Advertisements are delivered via Web pages, banner ads, and so forth. In this instance, the consumer can respond to the ad, modify it, expand it, or ignore it.

SPECIFIC REASONS FOR ADVERTISING

Let us go somewhat deeper and learn the varied reasons for using advertising as a tool. These reasons speak volumes about the multi-dimensional nature of advertising and its special importance:

1. *To announce a new product or service:* To promote new products, advertising becomes bold and dramatic. It should also convince us about the novelty. For new products, we need an initial splash of advertising but it has to be followed by sustained efforts.
2. *To expand, the to new buyers:* Here what has been successfully sold to one segment of the market is advertised to a new segment, Soft drinks are the craze for teenagers. But they are now promoted for children.
3. *To announce a modification:* Many consumer's products time and again are given a new lease of life by a certain product modification, e.g., Clinic Shampoo becomes Clinic Plus, or salt becomes iodised salt. Advertising has a role to play here.
4. *To announce a price change:* Price is used as key variable at times to boost sales. Reduced prices or discounts available on products become a matter of advertisement.
5. *To announce a new pack:* Advertisement in illustrations and photos identify a pack when a

pack design is changed the whole personality of the product changes. So this is announced through advertising.

6. *To make a special offer:* There are gifts and premiums that go with the product. There are introductory offers. There is a special offer in slack season.
7. *To invite enquiries:* Most industrial advertisements and many consumer product advertisements (especially of services) bring forth enquiries from potential customers. Coupons are generally employed to bring the enquiries.
8. *To sell direct*: Mail order selling of books, sports goods, textiles, gift items, etc., is conducted through pamphlets called direct mailings.
9. *To test a medium:* Couponed advertisement placed in an untried media tests the effectiveness of that media.
10. *To announce the location of stockist:* The list of dealers appended to an advertisement supports the dealers' selling efforts.
11. *To obtain stockists:* This is a pull strategy. The consumers demand an advertised product from the retailers. These in turn approach the wholesalers, who then solicit agency from the company. This strategy is very much successful for new products. However, for other products, which are not available, it is not wise to advertise them.
12. *To educate' customers:* We come across both informative and persuasive advertising. The informative variety is more acceptable such a copy is educative it gives explanation about and product or service. People need education about air travel, foreign jaunts, packaged tours and tourist places.
13. *To maintain sales:* Advertising continues for the whole life of a product. Introductory advertising is

of course heavy. But then to maintain sales, moderate advertising is necessary. Absence of total advertising may lead to extinction, of a product.

14. *To challenge competition:* A campaign may be designed to take on the competitor. Such challenges may be in the form of sales promotion methods or a comparison by a competitor of your product with his product.
15. *To remind:* though it sounds like sales maintenance, it is somewhat distinct. Small items like milk, bread toffees, chocolates, éclairs, blades, tea etc. are purchased repeatedly in small units. Reminder advertising asks the buyers to stick to the same brand; it also encourages the repurchases of the brand. Slogans and jingles are a great help here. Sometimes this genre makes up our mind or a particular brand whose need may arise in future.
16. *To get back lost sales:* Sometimes a company reduces advertising abruptly and suffers a loss in terms of sales. Again we will have to arrange a special campaign to get back the lost sales. Mail advertising is used for trade. Special sales promotion methods are used.
17. *To please stockiest:* The goods must move from shelf. There should be rapid turnover of stock, since the margins are small. It is like re-using the capital. Advertising thus helps the stockiest to achieve this. It makes them inclined to make the shelf space available. Direct mails are used to sell in, and consumer advertising and sales promotion are used to sell out.
18. *To please the sales force:* Effective advertisement improves the moral of the sales force. Advertising support also supplements their selling efforts.

19. *To recruit staff:* Advertising is a source of recruitment. It may be a small classified advertisement or a prominent display advertisement.
20. *To attract investors:* Financial advertising has come of age. There are special agencies who handle this. It makes you favourable towards an investment or a donation. It gives the details of returns on this investment or the social benefits of the donation. Share and securities issues are floated with sound advertisement support
21. *To export*: Media abroad are quite different. There are trade fairs etc. International advertising requires expert guidance. Export advertising without market research and media research can be a costly failure.
22. *To announce trading results:* It is also financial advertising. Extracts of chairman's speech are published in the media. In a way, he is announcing the financial results. The speech is well edited and well illustrated.

Advertisement interacts directly with other elements of marketing mix. It is basically a communication's to achieve marketing objectives. It is meant to bring something deliberately to the—notice of someone else—this is the semantic truth of the word, which comes from the French word "avertir" to notify Nicoll—Advertising is one element of the integrated marketing effort. The relative importance of the advertising would depend on: types of the products and form ‹ f marketing.

BENEFITS OF ADVERTISING

It is true that it pays to advertise. Advertising is a constructive activity. It helps the manufacturers to keep down the production costs by giving them economies of scale resulting from increased sale and hence increased production. It helps them to use the un-used capacity by stimulating demand. Advertising informs the consumers about the salient features and availability of the products.

- Advertising gives an image to the products of the manufacturers. In the market place, really speaking it is not the products, which compete, but the product images, which compete.
- Advertising pre-sells the products to distributors and so it is supportive to a salesman's visit.
- Advertising is an essential part of total promotional mix and promotion is an important part of the marketing mix.
- Advertising makes a psychological impact on the consumers and so gives them greater satisfaction on the use of products. People buy not a lip-stick, but the concept of an out-going, gorgeous, passionate woman. They also do not buy a computer but a solution to their complex problems. Thus what the product really stands for it is made known to us through advertising.
- Advertising affects our attitudes and values. It projects an image of self, which we aspire to. Advertising of life-style is making our target audience respond to it positively. Who would not like to be fun loving, outward-oriented, young socialites sailing in a group on sea, enjoying with Thumps Up which is Toofani Thunda?
- Advertisement thus gives all the benefits to manufacturer by selling—directly or indirectly. It can create a new demand, stimulate an existing demand, or even destroy a demand. Much of its value is drawn from its positive impact on demand function.

- Advertising makes distribution easier. It also reduces distributor's cost. They sell a highly advertised brand at a lesser price, and so a lesser margin. It builds up repeat sales for distributors. Remember how Photophone industries created market for their new product launch: Hot Shot camera by an effective advertising campaign. The words Khatak, Khatak and the slogan just aim and shoot still linger in our memory.
- Advertising renders invaluable help in launching new products. It has been proved time and again. Balearic's Promise was launched successfully against Colgate's monopoly of this market, thanks to imaginative advertising. Recently. Babool has repeated history. Even Vicco Vajradanti became established as a herbal product of *'ayurvedic jadibuti'* and *'kudrat's anmol khazana'* by advertising.

  The wholesaler and retailer find it easier to sell an advertised product. Good Knight Mosquito Repellent Heater and mats were successfully sold by all retailers, thanks to heavy and effective commercials and press advertising.
- Advertising benefits the customers. They come to know about the products and product information. They get the information about the product availability.
- Advertising makes mass distribution possible. Advertising makes the consumers aspire to higher and higher things in life making this life a saga of continuous struggle to acquire what we don't have. It expands the markets.
- Advertising creates markets for new products. It makes us aware of new uses of old products. Consumer gets post-purchase satisfaction. Because there is advertising, consumer gets a wide choice. It makes competitive economy possible.

ADVERTISING AND MANUFACTURERS

There is justification in the adage, 'it pays to advertise', because of the following advantages enjoyed by the advertiser i.e. manufacturer or producer:

1. *Increased sales*: The main objective of any advertiser is to increase the sale volume of the product by increasing, or creating the demand of the product. Goods produced on mass scale are not or cannot be sold at their own. The new product should be introduced to the consumers so that they can have knowledge about the product and may think to purchase it. So mass persuasion is necessary and done through advertising. By repeating advertising, the manufacturers are not only retain the existing sales but they can expand the market for their products by attracting new consumers to their products and by suggesting new uses for them. It can help achieving the main objective of the business i.e. minimum cost and maximum profits by multiplying the sales volume through advertising.
2. *Steady demand*: The sales volume once attained by dint of advertising should be established through repeated advertising. Regular and frequent advertising helps to ensure a more loyal cliental and more regular and even flow of sales by keeping the name, location, products and services of the selling house constantly before the public. Advertising also smoothens the seasonal demand of many products by suggesting alternative uses of the product to the public so that it gives up its seasonal character and the demand prevails and over the whole year. The innovation of cold coffee cold tea for use during summer has helped in increasing the demand of these beverages evening that season.

3. *Quick turnover and smaller inventories:* A well-organised advertising campaign creates a highly responsive market, which in turn ensures faster and greater turnover of the goods. This, in turn, results in lower inventories in relation to sales being carried on by the manufacturers. It reduces investment in working capital and increases the profitability of the concern.
4. *Lower costs*: Advertising leads to lower costs of marketing and production due to increased volume of sales. As the turnover gets increased in volume and pace, the distribution or marketing cost is averaged low because of savings in warehousing, transportation and order cost. It also reduces the per unit cost of advertising. The increase in the sales volume necessitates increased volume of production thus resulting in lowering the average cost of production due to reduction in various overheads.
5. *Greater dealer interest:* The dealers who sell advertised goods are greatly assisted by the advertisement made by the manufacturers. Advertising creates demand of the product, which is shared by every retailer without spending a penny on advertisement. It is not much bothered about pushing up the sales of goods already advertised by the manufacturers. So, they evince more interest in advertised products. There is one more reason for dealer interest. As the consumer knows much about the product before he/she enters a shop, the dealer is not required to persuade the customer for selling the product. Thus, advertising by manufacturers pays to dealers also and manufacturer is benefited by it.
6. *Creation of goodwill*: Advertising creates goodwill for the manufacturers of quality products because of

constantly associating the name of the manufacturers with the standard products. Goodwill is a valuable asset for the business and he may get advantage of this asset while introducing a new product in the market with confidence as well as in getting more and more orders for the existing products. Tata, Relaince. Godrej, Modi, Birla, etc. all sell the whole range of their products only on the strength of their goodwill.

7. *It controls product prices*: By means of advertisement, the whole sale and retail prices can be controlled to a great extent because the greedy wholesalers and retailers do not dare overcharge the needy customers which they can do if the company does not advertise the price of the product. The manufacturers have to face trouble of dwindling sales by the activities of swindlers if they, do not announce or print the retail price for the consumers. By advertising the prices in the newspaper or on radio or television or printing it on the wrappers of the product, the manufacturer saves the consumers from being exploited by the retailers and thus saves his/her own interest also.

Advertising and Sales Force

Advertising and personal selling are two aspects of promotional strategy. They are interrelated, inseparable and supplementary to each other. Advertising supports the sales force of the company in the following manner:

1. *It creates a colourful background:* A salesman may be well-trained, active, tactful and versatile in his mission of distribution. Salesmanship is alone like singing without accompaniment of orchestra. Background music makes even lifeless song lively, attractive and melodious. Thus, in marketing the product, background music is provided by the

advertising. Thus advertisement assists the sales force amply as it creates a fertile ground to sow the seeds to reap the rich harvest in the form of increased volume of sales. In this way, advertising prepares the necessary background for the efforts of salesman. When a salesman visits the prospective customers, he has just to converse for a product with which the consumer may already have been familiarised.

2. *Advertising curtails the burden of tedious job*: Without Advertising, the task of salesman becomes irksome and difficult and he has to bear the burden of his task plus the task of publicity and advertising. It, then, becomes a sort of mono-acting. Publicity introduces the product, arouses interest in the prospective buyers and creates confidence in them. Salesman when meets the customer, finds a ground well prepared by the advertising. It makes his task quite easier and simpler. The advertising supplements and supplants his functioning and makes the work of salesman more productive.

Advertising and Consumers

The ultimate aim of marketing of goods is to satisfy the needs of the ultimate customer. The advertising is a means towards this end. Advertising helps the consumers in the following ways:

1. *A guiding force in making purchase decisions:* Advertising helps the consumers in taking decisions regarding the merits and demerits of various products of the kind, special features like prices, quality etc., of products from various producers because advertising disseminates useful information regarding products of different manufacturers. In this way, it guides the customer to go in for a particular product. A number of

varieties in the market creates confusion in the minds of the consumer and he is to make a choice out of them by using the information made available to his through advertisement.

2. *Improvement in quality*: Goods are generally advertised under brand names. When an advertisement appears in the brand name, it imprints an image of the product on the mind of the consumer that it would be better than the other brands of the same goods available in the market. If the use of the product advertised confirms his expectation, a repeat order can be expected. It will, thus, earn a favourable and nice reputation for the manufacturer resulting in more and more attraction of customers. The customer recognises the goods with the brand name as, every brand stands for a quality; it is a mark of value, a symbol of guarantee and reasonable price. The manufacturer's, thus prompted to maintain and, if possible, improve the quality of his brand so that the confidence of the customers can be maintained. On the other hand, if the quality of the brand does not confirm to customer's expectation, brand will lose its market very soon. So advertiser is very sincere in maintaining and improving the quality of the product.

3. *Elimination of unnecessary intermediaries:* By advertising the goods, a manufacturer comes in the direct touch of the customers. On the basis of improved quality, the manufacturer gets reputation in the market. In this process, the number of middlemen whose margins increase the price, are reduced. It benefits manufacturer and consumers both. On the one hand, it will increase the profits for the manufacturer and on the other hand, will reduce the prices of goods for the consumers.

4. *Education of consumers:* There is truth in saying that advertising is an educational and dynamic principle. Advertising aims at educating the buyers about new and new products and their alternative uses. It will, thus, bring in new ways of life to the people at large and prompt them to give up their old habits and inertia. Advertising, thus, paves the way to better standard of living.
5. *Better quality goods at cheaper prices:* As we have discussed earlier that advertising ensures better and improved quality of goods to consumers. It also assures the better quality goods at cheaper rates to consumers because:
   I Mass advertised goods are produced and distributed in large quantity and thus bring reduction in production and distribution costs to producer.
   (ii) Unnecessary middlemen are eradicated from the channel of distribution.
6. *Consumers' surplus:* Advertising increases the utility of the product. It points out and emphasizes the quality of the product and leads consumers to appreciate more strongly the utility of such goods. As such, the consumers may be willing to pay even more for certain products, which appear to have higher utility to them. If these products are available at original prices, there will naturally be certain amount of consumers' surplus in terms of increased satisfaction or pleasure derived from these products.

ADVERTISING AND SOCIETY

The merits of advertising to the society can be discussed under following heads:

1. *Existence of the press*: At the beginning of advertising, advertisement generally occupied some odd nooks and corners in the newspapers. But the present situation is just the reverse. Modern civilisation is sustained by the press and the press is sustained by advertisements. Journals, newspapers, magazines, periodicals etc., all look to advertisement for their support and sustenance. Now the whole press exists only due to the funds generated by the advertising. The cost of production of newspaper etc. would have been much higher in the absence of income from advertising.
2. *Change in motivation*: Advertising has completely changed the basis of human motivation. While in the past, people were much worried about the bare necessities of life and they lived and worked for them but now the whole emphasis has shifted to provide for themselves, the comforts, luxuries and semi-luxuries. Thus the motive force of fear (of going without necessities of life) has been replaced by desire.
3. *Better standard of living*: Advertising has been an effective tool contributing tremendously in raising the standard of living of the masses. Advertising creates a desire of possessing better and newer items through the education of buyers for better standard of living. Advertising gives a start and direct stimuli to consumer, which in turn lays pressure on production not only to produce more but also to produce better and quality products and services of varied nature.
4. *Encouragement to research*: Advertising encourages research and discovery of new products or new uses for existing products because it (advertising) assures their marketing and sufficient profits to

manufacturers. If manufacturer is not assured of marketing his new product at sufficient profits, he will not undertake the research work for discovering new products or new uses of existing products.

5. *Gainful employment opportunities*: Advertising provides gainful employment opportunities to a number of people directly or indirectly. Direct employment opportunities are available in specialised jobs requiring the services of experts and talented persons like artists, photographers, painters, writers, singers, actors, musicians, pressmen, executives and managing agencies etc. Indirectly, it helps to create employment avenues, as it stimulates production of goods be creating, sustaining and extending demand for different goods and services.
6. *Encouragement of artists*: As the advertising requires the services of a number of artists such as actors, story-writers, musicians, singers, photographers etc., they always get or have an opportunity to do some creative work to make the advertisement attractive and valuable for those whom it is meant for while earning their livelihood by putting ideas in them while designing of advertisements.
7. *Glimpse of national life*: Advertising acts as a mirror of nation life, which shows the country's way of life. It is, in fact, a running commentary of the way the people live and behave and thus reflects the customs, habits etc. of the countrymen. It may be looked as an indicator of some of the future trends in this regard.

IMPORTANCE OF ADVERTISING

All that advertisement has to do is to sell a product or

service. This the advertisement accomplishes by communicating properly and effectively, by communicating the right message, put across through brilliant and persuasive language, making use of appeals to different human motives. Advertisements sometimes do the sales job in a subtle and direct manner. They incline us favourably to the products, they affect our attitudes.

So advertising performs the economic function by being an art of persuasions. It is also helped by a science of layout, visualisation, print reproduction, special effects on films etc. Advertising has created wide markets. Sales information is conveyed to millions of people far and wide. This makes mass production and mass distribution possible. Advertising establishes a direct rapport with the buyers, with no middlemen in the way.

Advertising is a subject of study in journalism, mass communication and management schools. It is a profession which employees both creative and non-creative persons—persons as account executives, media planners, art directors, administrative heads, copywriters etc. It indirectly gives employment to a host of other functionaries like commercial artists, media employees, studio people, freelancers, street-walkers and talkers, radio and TV announcers, jingle singers, video production unit and what not.

Advertising is also an economic process it helps the products to become known, to facilitate ultimately an exchange between those who need the products and those who can satisfy this need. Advertising is: "in fact a part of marketing mix consisting of Four its (Product, Price, Promotion and Place}. Advertising not only markets the products, but also a corporate ethos, a corporate philosophy by giving memorable corporate stories reaching deeper into the public-psyche than a bare recitation of performance statistics.

2

BRANDING

Basically brands start off as products made out of certain ingredients. Over a period of time, brands are built through marketing activities and communications. They keep on acquiring attributes, core values and extended values.

Despite the branding, consumers may treat a certain product as a commodity like cement, since the price is the same for all the brands and all of them have established the same identity. To begin with, just a little value addition like packaging makes a commodity a brand but when all competitors do the same thing, there is the danger of the brand again switching back to its commodity status. Many consumers prefer lower priced generics, which are sufficiently satisfying.

Generic products are a challenge to high-priced brands and weaker brands. Some companies cut their prices to competitive with generics. It is desirable. As we have already observed, branding makes things easier for consumers to identify products and services. Brands ensure a comparable quality when products are repurchased. Brands simplify your shopping.

Choosing a commodity is far more complex than choosing a brand. Commodity selection is based on rational left-brain logic. Brands have emotive associations. They can be chosen on a more holistic basis involving parallel left and right brain processing. The firms find that brands can be advertised. The firms also get the advantage of recognition when brands are on the shelves of the retailers. There is no confusion between branded products amongst consumers. Branding makes price comparisons difficult. Good brands help build a corporate image. Branding gives added prestige to the marketer. Branding also gives legal protection to the seller. Brand loyalty protects a firm against competition. Branding enables a seller to segment the market.

The distributors prefer branding as an identification tool for vendors, as a convenient tool to handle the products, and as a guarantee to certain production standard. These are some of the factors which encourage sellers to brand their products though branding is a costly proposition, involving the costs of packaging, labeling, advertising and legal protections.

The firms have to carry out two onerous tasks once they decide to brand-promoting the brand and maintaining a constant quality. If these two requirements cannot be met, products are better left unbranded. Branding decision is related to the nature of the product and the trade channel is involved. The sophistication of the distribution channels is conducive to branding. The opening up of a vast national market also augurs well for branding. Brand development and personal disposable income have a positive correlationship.

SPONSORSHIP

The most important branding decision is about the sponsorship of the brand—whether it is going to be manufacturer's or national brand or it is going to be a middleman's brand. In countries like the US, this is a very important decision, owing to the presence of large departmental stores and super-markets. In India, now mass retailing has register its presence. Middleman's private brands in India are still restricted to co-operative superbazars and NCCF (National Consumer Co-operative Federation). Some retailers have brand names in the product category of sarees. In the US, manufacturers may produce some output under their own name, and some under distributor's level. Private label brands in the US wage a constant war with the national brand.

FRANCHISING

Franchising deals are therefore becoming the order of the day. There are many American companies who have shown interest in launching their brands in India by franchising like Walt Disney Consumer Products (WDCP) has entered into licensing agreements with many prominent marketers for the use of its Disney characters on a range of products. The computer education Network, NIIT has opened 93 centres across the country in a span of 10 years. Out of these, 7 centres are run by NIIT itself, while 64 are franchisees.

Franchising has reduced the need of large investments. The franchisee gains by tying up with an established brand. Financing becomes easier, since goodwill of the present company backs up the franchisee. The marketing costs are borne by the franchiser. The franchisee has a finger on the local pulse. He can adopt faster to market needs. Holiday Inn Worldwide earns 3 per cent royalty on gross room revenue. It takes care of the marketing and advertising costs for all its franchisees. Growth of franchising is related to growth of branding. For high-income consumers, brands are reflectors for showing their affluence and status.

The company has to choose its brand name strategy. Each product can have a separate brand name, or one family name can be extended to all the products. Philips follows the family brand name strategy. Unilever brands the individual products. Let us consider the pros:

Family Brand

(*a*) It is cost effective in as much as it reduces product launch costs and also the promotional expenses incurred on a continuing basis. The success of one brand when well promoted gives a push to the entire product line. Management of trade channel also is easier.

(*b*) For products of uneven quality, this approach is a dicey proposition. Even in markets showing variations in consumer profiles, this approach is not useful.

(*c*) Each product is denied a special identity, which can go a long way to make it click. Like Nokia is a corporate or family brand. There is no subbranding and the individual products are merely defined by numeric descriptors such as 5110, and even these do not appear on the product itself. Yet, the brand has leapfrogged most of its competitors like Motorola and Ericsson. Even in technology-based businesses, a company can have a brand strategy.

Individual Brand

(*a*) Individual brand invokes associations and imageries. These psychological factors influence the buying decision.

(*b*) Even if the product fails, the effects are restricted to that product only. They are not transferred to the whole product line.

(*c*) Costlier strategy.

(*d*) No benefit to the brand of the organisation's reputation.

Modified Strategy

These days' companies tend to brand the products individually, but also give prominence to the company's name or logo in all promotional efforts and product packaging. Some companies adopt brand extension strategy, by introducing similar or dissimilar products, e.g., Nirma toilet soaps. Some organisations decide several brand names of the same product where each brand has its own following. The brands compete amongst themselves. Soap manufacturers follow this strategy. Alries and Jack Trout are against brand extensions. In their opinion, brands are not dying—the companies are killing them through mindless line extensions. When a company line extends, it weakens itself. Product categories can be given extensions, e.g., gel pastes, detergent ultras, puri-gerators. Telephone directory reclassified becomes Yellow Pages. It is more than mere positioning. It is creating a new product category with just an extra push. Tinker in the lab and let the brand or product plus emerge, e.g., gel, cologne soap, micro system, germi check etc.

The choice of an individual brand name is the next important decision. The choice is not so easy. There are really few good brand names. As a wit has aptly remarked, "Searching for a brand name is like search for a wife—there are lots of choices, but the best ones have already been taken." Sometimes, brand names are based on a person's name, e.g., Honda Estee Lauder, Khaitan. Brand names can be based on locations, e.g., Indian Airline, Kentucky Fried Chicken. Brand names can suggest an important product attribute, e.g., Duracell. These are brand names which suggest a life-style, e.g., Fleet Footers. EXXON and Kodak have an interesting history behind them. When ESSO found it necessary to change its name, the computer was fed with various vowels and consonantal combinations, and 44,990 four letter and 500,000 five-letter combinations came out. EXXON was finally chosen because it is distinctive and has graphic design possibilities. Kodak was coined by George Eastman in 1888 because he liked the letter 'K' and wanted a name which could not be misspelt.

CHARACTERISTICS OF A GOOD BRAND NAME

A good brand name should possess as many of the following characteristics as possible:

(i) *It should be distinctive:* The market is filled with overworked names and over-used symbols. A unique and distinctive symbol is not only easy to remember but also a distinguishing feature. "Northstar" shoes have a distinct name.

(ii) *It should be suggestive:* A well-chosen name or symbol should be suggestive of quality, or may be associated with superiority or a great personality. The name VIP Classic for travellers is suggestive of a superior quality for a distinct class of people. Promise is suggestive of an assurance of tooth health.

(iii) *It should be appropriate:* Many products are surrounded by a certain mystique in the minds of the consumers. Carefree is an appropriate brand name of a sanitary towel.

(iv) *It should be easy to remember:* It should be easy to read, pronounce and spell. Tide, Surf, Coca Cola are examples of such brand names.

(v) *It should be adaptable to new products:* Videocon is as good brand name for TVs and VCRs but when it is extended to refrigerators and washing machines, some of the sales appeal is lost. Hotline was a good name for gas stoves, but definitely not a suitable name for TVs.

(vi) It should be registerable under the Indian laws of Trade Marks and Copyrights. Mostly a company develops several names for a product and makes a choice later after debate and discussion.

GENERIC USAGE OF BRAND NAMES

Sometimes, a brand name becomes so successful that it comes to be associated with a particular product category, e.g., Dalda is a brand name commonly used for any vanaspati ghee. The brand names then do not remain distinct and become generic. Cellophane, nylon, fibreglass, celluloid, Kerosene and aspirin have thus become generic. Xerox and Band Aid are not yet legally generic, but they have been so well promoted that many people just use them generically. Though each firm strives to have a popular and preferred brand names, it does not like it becoming generic. It is a tight-rope walk. To protect against such generic use, a brand name can be combined with a company's name, e.g., Eastman Kodak. A brand name can be combined with a generic name, e.g., Dacron polyester, Dabur Chyavanprash.

A brand that becomes generic becomes a product category, and no longer remains a brand. Frigidaire is GE's brand. But now well call any refrigerator a 'fridge' so it has become generic. Other well-positioned brands have overtaken Frigidaire, and it is no longer a market-leader. Dalda Vanaspati has become generic. It is now again trying to lose its generic label. Though consumer asks a product by the generic name, he ends up buying a brand that offers attractive benefits. The generic brand sits on the shelf.

BRANDING STRATEGY

Small business owners need to find ways to differentiate themselves and appeal to their target audience in new ways, and that means building a brand.

Enterprise Magazine

1. *Treat your customers with the utmost respect:* Gone are the days when companies could patronise their consumers. People these days are more creative, more selective, and they feel more empowered. Witness for example the increased brand promiscuity in financial services. People are also deluged with information and opportunity. The brands they select and build relationships with are those who treat them as intelligent adult partners, not witless infantile drones. If you want these people as your customers, your branding strategy must acknowledge this.
2. *Be a customer-focused brand, but not a customer-led one:* This doesn't contradict the previous point. People need to feel that organisations are providing them with products that deliver real benefits, and with services that help make their lives easier. But they won't be your creative department when it comes to working out exactly what these things are. That is your responsibility. Remember, no one begged for alcopops, or premium adult ice-cream. But they sure picked up on these things when they were dreamed up and offered to them. A customer focused brand should pre-empt customer desire for these products through knowledge of their customers.
3. *Don't get obsessive about a slogan:* When trying to build a brand, people often get obsessed with creating strap lines, and coming up with catchy signature phrases. Nice if you stumble upon a great one, like "Just do it". But they're not necessary to build a great brand. Sceptical? OK then, name me the "lines" for brands like: Microsoft, Maruti, Vodafone, Virgin Atlantic, McDonald's, etc.

4. *Remember your brand's place in people's lives:* People are busy. They don't respond well to brands which have lost that human perspective, and are the equivalent of the saloon-bar bore. However, they do respond well to a brand that clearly "knows its place" in people's lives—a brand that spells accessibility, flexibility, humanity, and often a sense of humour. Allow the customer to have a major say in how and when he drives the brand relationship.
5. *ESPs (Emotional Selling Propositions)are more powerful than USPs (Unique Commerce Propositions) in brand building:* It's difficult to create a genuine unique selling point these days. It's even more difficult to keep it unique. If it's a good one, the competition will follow. There's a further issue—own label brands are often stronger than branded brands.
6. *A brand needs a seat at the high table:* You won't build the brand you want unless the entire company is aligned. And that's not as simple as it should be. First, there's the over-arching responsibility of every chief executive to maximise shareholder value. Which all too often is measured only as far as the next six month's numbers, not in terms of prospects for the next six years. Hats off here to the Halifax, for reworking the interest structure in favour of its account holders. That needed boardroom support. There's a second point here, which becomes evident if you talk to hi-tech companies. The boffins are invariably doing extremely clever stuff. Problem is, this is often entirely tangential to their prospective customer's day-to-day lives. Far better to ensure all development work is within a clear brand agenda.
7. *If your own people don't get it, no one will:* A simple point that's often overlooked—especially in service companies. Real brand reputation is created at the

point of delivery. If your own people don't know the strategy and agenda and understand the central role they play in building your brand, it won't be delivered. So have very clear internal processes which inform and involve the front-line staff.

8. *Brands are primarily what you do, not what you say:* It's more than just having motivated people at the point of delivery. It's also about demonstrating the brand's commitment—launching new products that make the point. Examples include the BA flat-bed in long-haul business class, and Tesco's returns policy. These can reach beyond the traditional provision of better products and services. "Good citizen" sponsorships which are clearly of value to the communities they serve can be very potent in building a customer conscious brand. A standard-bearer was Texaco, with its child safety activity in the late 80s.

9. *Be consistent with your brand's presentation:* There's been a lot of talk about integration. Quite right too. Strong brand building needs cohesive communications and delivery. Yet the most likely breakdown of the alchemy that represents a powerful brand is inconsistency of approach. Not only mismatch between rhetoric and reality, but also different messages, with different tones, personality and core values disseminated and therefore consumed through different channels. And there are now plenty of those channels. Online and offline, paid and unpaid media, broadcast and narrowcast, the list goes on.

10. *Stick with it:* Brand-building needs to transcend the rational. It is a headand-heart thing. If there was a logical equation, everyone would be brand leader. However, it's not physics—it's alchemy. Resist the temptation to chop and change. Evolve, progress,

innovate, grow—but always remember to nurture the brand.

Brand Strategy Decisions

A company has four choices in respect of its brand strategy:

(i) *Line extensions:* Extend the existing brand name in the existing product category.

(ii) *Brand extensions:* Extend the brand name to new product category.

(iii) *Multiple brands:* Have new brand names in the same product category.

(iv) *New brands:* Invent a new brand name for a new product category.

Most of the new products in the day-to-day use and grocery products are line extensions. A few are brand extensions. A few new brand names appear in both multiple brand strategy and new brand strategy.

Line extensions

Here the company introduces additional items in the same product category, keeping the brand name same. The additional items may be of a different size. There may be a new form, say Liquid Lifebuoy Soap. The additional item can be of different colour say, a lilac soap instead of a white soap. The package may be different, say a satchet of a shampoo. Some additional flavours can be introduced, say Brown & Polson Custard Powder is now available in chocolate and with elaichi flavour. There may be added ingredients, say, Lifebuoy Gold. Lux is available in three skin types, say for normal skin, dry skin and oily skin, making it "your kind of soap for your kind of skin." Line extensions can be innovative, or "me-too" or may be voidfilling. Most of the new product activity is of line extension type. Line extensions offer a variety to the customers. An advantage can be taken of consumer's latent need. Or else, a competitor is to be matched in terms of its offer. Line extensions also allow a company to command more shelf-space at the retail level.

Line extensions can be made available through a specific mix of trade channels, e.g., lower end products are available at general stores and higher end products at a few specialised outlets.

Line extension, though very popular, is not without its drawbacks. The specific meaning of a brand might be lost by heavy extensions. Ries and Trout are against line extensions. Today, Coke in India means a 300 ml, 500 ml and 1 litre bottle of the real thing. Again, a can may be introduced. Perhaps, there may be a diet Coke also. All this may become confusing. Besides, what is the guarantee that all these will have sales sufficient to cover the costs? Even additional sales may be at the cost of other items in the line. Line extensions work only if the sales are taken away from the competitors. Mostly, they eat up the sales of our own brands.

Brand Extensions

An existing brand name is extended to a product being launched in a new product category. Honda is a brand in the field of motorbikes. The same brand name is given to products in the field of lawnmowers, and marine engines. Brand extension works well for rubbing off the success of established brand names to new products. The new product, therefore, finds easy acceptance. However, if the new product is not satisfactory in performance, it might affect the reparations of the company's other products. Most of the times, brand name may not be appropriate for the new product category. While brand extending, it advisable to see how the associations of the parent brand are consistent with the extended brand.

Multiple Brands

The strategy is employed to saturate the market. Additional brands are introduced to cater to the different segments, e.g., P&G's Tide is for soiled clother and Draft is for gently clothes. P & G produces nine different brands of detergents. Sometimes, flanker brands are introduced to protect the major brand, e.g., high-priced Seiko watches are protected by introducing lowpriced Pulsar watches, which are flanker brands. Multiple brands offer us price flexibility. A competitor's' fighting brands' are so priced that they beat those of the competitor. This way the main brand is protected, and its price is not cut. Multiple brand strategy may not allow the company's resources to be focused. They may get dissipated over a large number of brands. Besides, if each brand has a small market share, the overall profitability may get affected. Our brands should affect the competitor's brands, and not the other brands of our own-Sometimes, a company gets a legacy of new brands in the process of acquisition. Thus Coca Cola got the Thums Up, Gold Spot and Limca brands.

In India, consumer durable are showing stagnant demand. Companies have to launch several brands at different price points either with one mother brand as umbrella brand, and several differentiated sub-brands or a separate new brand like Evelux TV from BPL or Akai and Sansui from Videocon.

In the market place of today, there is a virtual marketing warfare where brands fight with one another on the basis of quality, reputation and market share. Marketing strategy to a large extent is defined by brand strategy. Multibranding approach is a measure adopted by many FMCG companies, followed by consumer durable and service sector companies to survive in the competitive environment.

A company must first identify its core brand, which delivers the largest volume and highest cash flow. In a sense, it is the market leader. Our effort should be directed towards the protection of this core brand, by creating one or more smaller product categories to protect the flanks, after strengthening the top and the rear with a slew of other aggressive products. HLL follows this strategy to market Lux by creating other soaps like Jai to product it. Colgate follows multibranding strategy to guard its main product Colgate Dental Cream.

Videocon protected itself by creating Bazooka as a top-of-the line product and introducing Toshiba. It protected the brand in all size and price categories by introducing private. Sansui protected its flanks. In this process, the core brand tends to get compressed over a medium-to-long-term period, leading to gain in the market share of other brands. But as the production capacities are shored up, the brand shares get fragmented, leading to an overall consolidation of the core brand. Multibranding can be practiced by segmenting the market on socio-economic parameters e.g. Raymond as a core brand is surrounded by Park Avenu for professional , Parx range of casuals for youth and manzoni, , to-of-the-line range of ties, suits, and jackets. Multi-branding is a strategy followed be big players.

New Brands

To make brand names more appropriate, a company puts a new brand name when it enters a new product category. A new brand again has to be built up, and this is quite expensive. It should be considered whether the sales and profits estimated for the new brand justify it.

ROLE OF BRAND

A brand does not merely satisfy a need of the consumer.

It is no use force-fitting a brand to the consumer. A consumer as such has aims, ambitions, motivations, drives and desires. Each consumer tries to satisfy the higher level needs after satisfying the basic needs. It is a desire to each, and a desire to have power that goals a consumer to higher and higher levels. A brand should be a means to empower the consumer—he should feel more powerful when he uses the brand. The emotional payoff of the brand should lead to enhancement of positive selfimage. Self-image can be improved when a consumer's intrinsic or extrinsic worth is enhanced. Intrinsic worth denotes a better feeling about oneself. Extrinsic worth means a better feeling of the consumer in the eyes of the world around him. Brand payoff should ensure that emotional payoff is exclusive and relevant. It takes a brand to its destination.

Regional Brands

- In India we come across many regional brands, which compete with the national brands in several product categories. A regional brand is unique to a particular region. Some brands remain regional on account of the constraints of resources. Some do so on account of their very provincial appeal.
- Regional brands are under assault by the national and transnational companies. They have started offering regional variants. Brands like Fights in processed food witness a number of brands from Nestle and Milkmaid gobbling up the market created by it.
- When a regional brand remains confined to a region, it faces the competition from the regional variant of a national brand. When regional brands venture to go national, they may over-leverage their meager resources. But there is not way they can afford to remain silent spectators. They should

extrapolate the regional model in spirit, and not in letter.

Attitude Brands

Body shop puts forward human body as an asset. Benetoon ads denote an irreverent attitude. MTV as a brand is thought of as one packed with rebelliousness of this generation. We have an 'honest shirt'. These brands do things differently. They jolt the customer who take notice of the brand.

In-Store Brands

Even you would have come across what are known as 'private label' brands. These are store brands.

— They are defined as a product line, which is owned, controlled, merchandised and sold by a specific retailer in its own stores. They enable a retailer to attain higher margins by providing higher value to the customers and by saving costs.

— They also increase a retailer's bargaining power with the suppliers of national brands. By being exclusive, private labels generate customer loyalty.

— We come across private levels in garments and foods. Shopper's Stop gets more than 15 per cent of its total sales through private label brands. Foodworld too has private label grocery brands.

— Private lablels should be more consumer-centric. They should fill-up the consumer need gaps. Retailers are quit close to the customer. They observe the shopping behaviour of the consumers. They are thus in a better position to design suitable products.

— A retailer who chooses to launch private labels becomes a marketer, and not merely a seller of products. It brings he whole brand building process in the organisation. Retailers can exercise flexibility in marketing these brands by adapting to change.

Brand and National Identity

In this wired world, brands are becoming global, but still they do maintain their original roots, e.g., Coke is an American brand and Mercedes Bens is a German brand. 'Brand's national identity is based on where that brand is created. We may make a Sony in India, but still it is a Japanese brand. A product can be manufactured and created anywhere but a brand has a national identity. However, national identity sometimes does not work to our advantage. American computers have strong positive national identity, but American cars are considered mediocre.

Aaker identifies four types of roles for the brands. A brand becomes a driver brand when it leads to the purchase decision. Here the brands represents the package of benefits a customer expects from the brand. The driver brand can be the basic brand or sub-brand or corporate brand or a combination. In a computer industry, Intel can be a driver brand, rather than the computer brand itself. In detergents, we have Surf Excel, and Excel becomes the driver brand owing to the presence of enzymes it suggests which the consumer is actually buying. In Bajaj Chetak, Bajaj is the driver brand as it represents reliability and performance Driver brands must be emphasized in promotion and packaging.

A brand plays the role of endorser also. Here it supports the driver brand and its claims. It thus lends credibility to the driver brand. Corporate brands are generally the endorser brands. A brand can be both a driver and endorser brand. In several courses, to being with corporate brand which supports a driver brand is usually used. Later, the corporate brand is withdrawn, when the driver brand can stand-alone.

BENEFITS OF BRANDING

It provides benefits to buyers and sellers:

To Buyer

- Help buyers identify the product that they like/dislike.
- Identify marketer.
- Helps reduce the time needed for purchase.
- Helps buyers evaluate quality of products especially if unable to judge products characteristics.
- Helps reduce buyers perceived risk of purchase.
- Buyer may derive a psychological reward from owning the brand, IE Rolex or Mercedes.

To Seller

- Differentiate product offering from competitors.
- Helps segment market by creating tailored images.
- Brand identifies the company's products making repeat purchases easier for customers.
- Reduce price comparisons.
- Brand helps firm introduce a new product that carries the name of one or more of its existing products, half as much as using a new brand, lower co. designs, advertising and promotional costs.

  Example, Gummy Savers.
- Easier cooperation with intermediaries with well known brands.
- Facilitates promotional efforts.
- Helps foster brand loyalty helping to stabilise market share.

3

ETHICS OF ADVERTISING

The field of advertising is extremely broad and diverse. In general terms, of course, an advertisement is simply a public notice meant to convey information and invite patronage or some other response. As that suggests, advertising has two basic purposes: to inform and to persuade, and—while these purposes are distinguishable—both very often are simultaneously present.

Advertising is not the same as marketing or public relations. In many cases, though, it is a technique or instrument employed by one or both of these. Advertising can be very simple—a local, even neighbourhood phenomenon—or it can be very complex, involving sophisticated research and multimedia campaigns that span the globe. It differs according to its intended audience, so that, for example, advertising aimed at children raises some technical and moral issues significantly different from those raised by advertising aimed at competent adults.

Not only are many different media and techniques employed in advertising; itself is of several different kinds: commercial advertising for products and services; public service advertising on behalf of various institutions, programmes, and causes; and—a phenomenon of growing importance today—political advertising in the interests of parties and candidates. Making allowance for the differences among the different kinds and methods of advertising, we intend what follows to be applicable to them all.

Advertisers are selective about the values and attitudes to be fostered and encouraged, promoting some while ignoring others. This selectivity gives the lie to the notion that advertising does no more than reflect the surrounding culture. For example, the absence from advertising of certain racial and ethnic groups in some multiracial or multi-ethnic societies can help to create problems of image and identity, especially among those neglected, and the almost inevitable impression in commercial advertising that an abundance of possessions leads to happiness and fulfilment can be both misleading and frustrating.

Advertising also has an indirect but powerful impact on society through its influence on media. Many publications and broadcasting operations depend on advertising revenue for survival. This often is true of religious media as well as commercial media. For their part, advertisers naturally seek to reach audiences; and the media, striving to deliver audiences to advertisers, must shape their content so to attract audiences of the size and demographic composition sought. This economic dependency of media and the power it confers upon advertisers carries with it serious responsibilities for both.

ETHICAL AND MORAL PRINCIPLES

The Second Vatican Council declared: "If the media are to be correctly employed, it is essential that all who use them know the principles of the moral order and apply them faithfully in this domain." The moral order to which this refers is the order of the law of human nature, binding upon all because it is "written on their hearts" and embodies the imperatives of authentic human fulfilment. For Christians, moreover, the law of human nature has a deeper dimension, a richer meaning. "Christ is the? Beginning' who, having taken on human nature, definitively illumines it in its constitutive elements and in its dynamism of charity towards God and neighbour." Here we comprehend the deepest significance of human freedom: that it makes possible an authentic moral response, in light of Jesus Christ, to the call "to form our conscience, to make it the object of a continuous conversion to what is true and to what is good."

The media of social communications have two options, and only two. Either they help human persons to grow in their understanding and practice of what is true and good, or they are destructive forces in conflict with human well being. That is entirely true of advertising. Against this background, then, we point to this fundamental principle for people engaged in advertising: advertisers—that is, those who commission, prepare or disseminate advertising—are morally responsible for what they seek to move people to do; and this is a responsibility also shared by publishers, broadcasting executives, and others in the communications world, as well as by those who give commercial or political endorsements, to the extent that they are involved in the advertising process.

If an instance of advertising seeks to move people to choose and act rationally in morally good ways that are of true benefit to themselves and others, persons involved in it do what is morally good; if it seeks to move people to do evil deeds that are self-destructive and destructive of authentic community, they do evil.

This applies also to the means and the techniques of advertising: it is morally wrong to use manipulative, exploitative, corrupt and corrupting methods of persuasion and motivation. In this regard, we note special problems associated with so-called indirect advertising that attempts to move people to act in certain ways—for example, purchase particular products—without their being fully aware that they are being swayed. The techniques involved here include showing certain products or forms of behavior in superficially glamorous settings associated with superficially glamorous people; in extreme cases, it may even involve the use of subliminal messages.

There are several moral principles that are particularly relevant to advertising. These are three: truthfulness, the dignity of the human person, and social responsibility.

Truthfulness in Advertising

Even today, some advertising is simply and deliberately untrue. Generally speaking, though, the problem of truth in advertising is somewhat more subtle: it is not that advertising says what is overtly false, but that it can distort the truth by implying things that are not so or withholding relevant facts. As Pope John Paul II points out, on both the individual and social levels, truth and freedom are inseparable; without truth as the basis, starting point and criterion of discernment, judgement, choice and action, there can be no authentic exercise of freedom. The Catechism of the Catholic Church, quoting the Second Vatican Council, insists that the content of communication be "true and —within the limits set by justice and charity—complete"; the content should, moreover, be communicated "honestly and properly."

To be sure, advertising, like other forms of expression, has its own conventions and forms of stylisation, and these must be taken into account when discussing truthfulness. People take for granted some rhetorical and symbolic exaggeration in advertising; within the limits of recognised and accepted practice, this can be allowable. But it is a fundamental principle that advertising may not deliberately seek to deceive, whether it does that by what it says, by what it implies, or by what it fails to say. The proper exercise of the right to information demands that the content of what is communicated be true and, within the limits set by justice and charity, complete. Included here is the obligation to avoid any manipulation of truth for any reason.

Dignity of the Human Person

There is an "imperative requirement" that advertising "respect the human person, his right duty to make a responsible choice, his interior freedom; all these goods would be violated if man's lower inclinations were to be exploited, or his capacity to reflect and decide compromised." These abuses are not merely hypothetical possibilities but realities in much advertising today. Advertising can violate the dignity of the human person both through its content—what is advertised, the manner in which it is advertised —and through the impact it seeks to make upon its audience. We have spoken already of such things as appeals to lust, vanity, envy and greed, and of techniques that manipulate and exploit human weakness. In such circumstances, advertisements readily become vehicles of a deformed outlook on life, on the family, on religion and on morality—an outlook that does not respect the true dignity and destiny of the human person.

This problem is especially acute where particularly vulnerable groups or classes of persons are concerned: children and young people, the elderly, the poor, the culturally disadvantaged. Much advertising directed at children apparently tries to exploit their credulity and suggestibility, in the hope that they will put pressure on their parents to buy products of no real benefit to them. Advertising like this offends against the dignity and rights of both children and parents; it intrudes upon the parent-child relationship and seeks to manipulate it to its own base ends. Also, some of the comparatively little advertising directed specifically to the elderly or culturally disadvantaged seems designed to play upon their fears so as to persuade them to allocate some of their limited resources to goods or services of dubious value.

Advertising and Social Responsibility

Social responsibility is such a broad concept that we can note here only a few of the many issues and concerns relevant under this heading to the question of advertising. The ecological issue is one. Advertising that fosters a lavish life style which wastes resources and despoils the environment offends against important ecological concerns. In his desire to have and to enjoy rather than to be and grow, man consumes the resources of the earth and his own life in an excessive and disordered way. Man thinks that he can make arbitrary use of the earth, subjecting it without restraint to his will, as though it did not have its own requisites and a prior God-given purpose, which man can indeed develop but must not betray.

As this suggests, something more fundamental is at issue here: authentic and integral human development. Advertising that reduces human progress to acquiring material goods and cultivating a lavish life style expresses a false, destructive vision of the human person harmful to individuals and society alike.

When people fail to practice a rigorous respect for the moral, cultural and spiritual requirements, based on the dignity of the person and on the proper identity of each community, beginning with the family and religious societies, then even material abundance and the conveniences that technology makes available will prove unsatisfying and in the end contemptible. Advertisers, like people engaged in other forms of social communication, have a serious duty to express and foster an authentic vision of human development in its material, cultural and spiritual dimensions. Communication that meets this standard is, among other things, a true expression of solidarity. Indeed, the two things—communication and solidarity—are inseparable, because, as the Catechism of the Catholic Church points out, solidarity is "a consequence of genuine and right communication and the free circulation of ideas that further knowledge and respect for others."

CODE FOR COMMERCIAL ADVERTISING ON DOORDARSHAN

This code was presented to Parliament in mid-1987. It incorporates the Indecent Representation of Women Act and the Consumer Act, both of which were passed by parliament in 1986. It suggests 33 Do's and Don'ts for advertisers. Here are some of them: Advertisements should conform to laws and should not offend against morality, decency and the religious susceptibilities of people.

The success of advertising depends on public confidence and no practice should be permitted which tends to impair this. The director-general shall be the sole judge of the code

The following advertisements should not be permitted:

1. Ads, which deride any race, caste, colour, creed and nationality or are against the Directive Principles or the Constitution.

2. Ads, which tend to incite people to crime or cause order or adversely affect friendly relations with foreign states.
3. Ads, which exploit national emblem, any part of the constitution, or the person/personality of national leaders or state dignitaries.
4. No advertisement shall be presented as news.
5. Ads, which have any relation to religion, political or industrial dispute.
6. Ads, which promote chit funds, moneylenders, jewellery, fortune letters, foreign goods, and private saving schemes.
7. Guaranteed goods will have to be made available to Director-General of Doordarshan for inspection if necessary.
8. No disparaging or derogatory remarks of other products or comparison with them should be made.
9. Ads, which portray women as passive or submissive.
10. Ads which are likely to startle viewers, such as gunfire, sirens, bombardments, screams, and raucous laughter.

As we know that Advertising establishes a link between the manufacturer and the consumer. It is a form of mass communication.

- Through advertising, the advertiser reaches a vast number of consumers, and makes his product known to them.
- Advertising makes it possible for the manufacturer to introduce new ideas and new products. Had it not been for advertising, we would not have accepted many products.

- Advertising keeps the consumers well informed about the products and services – styles, features, sizes, colours, specifications, prices, availability, instructions for use etc.
- Advertising has an educative role to play. It keeps the consumers conversant with the use of the products especially household appliances, capital goods etc.
- Advertising expands markets, builds up volumes, gives a market share and profitability, and reduces prices.
- Advertising makes product adoption process smooth. It sells corporate ethos and builds up corporate identity.

Colley lists fifty-two possible objectives of advertising in his well-known book Defining Advertising Goals for Measured Results (DAGMAR). For a manufacturer, advertising conveys information to his customers, persuades his customer and reminds them about the product. Of course, how advertising performs depends on other marketing factors.

Advertising Benefits the Consumers

Advertising has made its presence felt after the war years when buyers armed with the purchasing power had the capacity to buy not the will to buy. Advertising created that will and converted it into an effective demand.

Advertising became one of the essential ingredients of business—it was used to balance the production and consumption problem. So firstly you have to understand the problem and then convey the solution to it like if your problem is dandruff. For that I have an anti-dandruff shampoo. And similarly if you have a problem of dry hair, and shampoo for dry hair is a solution. He is trying to choose an investment channel. There is fixed deposit, as well as unfixed deposit. There is a banking problem at night. So we have electronic banking machines.

— Advertising guides the consumers in his product choices. It gives the information about the product, the benefits it offers, the availability and the price.

— Advertising is a philosopher also. It makes us aware of many socially relevant causes like dowry, energy conservation, loss prevention, social forestry etc. Advertising is thus a friend, philosopher and guide of the consumers.

— Advertising at times describes a product, at times narrates a story or an experience, and at times educates a consumer.

— It is a time saver for the consumers. It also gives the consumers promised performance, a promised quality. It gives cost benefits.

— It delivers a standard of living. It is a business worth several crores.

— It is a profession in which many are employed. It generates indirect employment by expanding the market.

— Advertising contributes to consumer welfare. It helps consumers in a variety of ways. It tells what to buy, how to buy, where to buy, and why to buy. It gives valuable price information. Some critics brand advertising as parasitical. They say you produce anything worthwhile, and it will sell (e.g., the world will beat a path to the better mouse-trap). No, this is not true. No one has now the time to be an explorer.

Today, we all are influenced by advertising. Advertising does not force us to make particular choices. It persuades us to do so.

ADVERTISING STANDARDS COUNCIL OF INDIA (ASCI)

The Advertising Standards Council of India (ASCI) has formulated a code for the advertising of tobacco products, which will be implemented from October 1. It covers all media from television to print to outdoor to new electronic media including the Internet, e-mail, pagers and CDROMs.

India Cable Ordinance

Main features

1. No person shall operate a cable television network unless he is registered as a cable operator.
2. No person shall transmit or re-transmit through a cable service any programme or advertisement unless such programme or advertisements is in conformity with the prescribed programme and advertisement code. However this will not be applicable to foreign satellite channels which can be received without the use of any specialised gadgets or decoders.
3. Every cable operator using a dish antenna or television receiver only shall re-transmit at least two Doordarshan satellite channels of his choice through the cable service. The Doordarshan channels shall be retransmitted without any deletion or alteration of any programme transmitted on such channels.
4. Within three years of the establishment and publication of the Indian Standard by the Bureau of Indian Standards all operations will use only such equipment which conforms to the Indian Standards.
5. Every cable operator shall ensure that the cable TV network being operated by him does not interfere

in any way, with the functioning of the authorised telecommunication systems.

6. Any programme which is likely to create hatred or ill-will between different religions, racial, linguistic regional or castes or communities or is prejudicial in maintaining harmony among such groups or which is likely to disturb the public tranquillity could be prohibited by the State or Central Government.
7. The operation of cable TV network in any area can be banned by the Central Government.
8. Each cable operator shall maintain a register for each month in the prescribed form indicating the channels/ programmes relayed.

Programme Code

No programme shall be carried in the cable service which:

(a) Offends against good taste or decency;

(b) Contains criticism of friendly countries;

(c) Contains attack on religions or communities or visuals or words contemptuous of religious groups or which promote communal attitudes;

(d) Contains anything obscene, defamatory, deliberate false and suggestive innuendoes and half truths;

(e) Is likely to encourage or indicate violence or contain anything amounting to contempt of court;

(f) Contains aspirations against the integrity of the President and the judiciary

(g) Contains anything affecting the integrity of the Nation;

(h) Contains anything affecting the integrity of the Nation;

Advertising Code

1. Advertising carried in the cable service shall be so designed as to conform to the laws of the country and should not offend morality, decency and religious susceptibilities of the subscribers.
2. No advertisements shall be permitted which:
   (i) derides any race, caste, colour, creed or nationality.
   (ii) is against any provision of the Constitution of India.
   (iii) tends to incite people to crime, cause disorder or violence, or breach of law or glorifies violence or obscenity in any way.
   (iv) presents criminality as desirable.
   (v) exploits the national emblem, or any part of the Constitution or the person or personality of a national leader or a State dignitary.
   (vi) in its depiction of women violates the Constitutional guarantees to all citizens. In particular no advertisement shall be permitted which projects a derogatory image of women. Women must not be portrayed in a manner that emphasises passive, submissive qualities and encourages them to play a subordinate, secondary role in the family and society. The cable operator shall ensure that the portrayal of the female form in the programmes carried in his cable service, is tasteful and aesthetic, and is within established norms of good taste and decency.
   (vi) exploits social evils like dowry, child marriage.
3. No advertisement shall be permitted the objects whereof are wholly or mainly of a religious or

political nature; advertisements must not be directed towards any religious or political end.

4. The goods or service advertised shall not suffer from any defect or deficiency as mentioned in Consumer Protection Act. 1986.
5. No advertisement shall contain references which are likely to lead the public to infer that the product advertised or any of its ingredients has some special or miraculous or supernatural property or quality, which is difficult of being proved.
6. The picture and the audible matter of the advertisement shall not be excessively 'loud'.
7. No advertisement which endangers the safety of children or creates in them any interest in unhealthy practices or shows them begging or in an undignified or indecent manner shall not be carried in the cable service.
8. Indecent, vulgar, suggestive, repulsive or offensive themes or treatment shall be avoided in all advertisements.
9. No advertisements which violates the standards or practice for advertising agencies as approved by the Advertising Agencies Association of India, Mumbai, from time to time shall be carried in the cable service.
10. All advertisements should be clearly distinguishable from the programme and should not interfere with the programme viz, use of lower part of screen to carry captions, static or moving alongside the programme.

Code for Commercial Advertising

Government means Government of India. 'Director

General' means the Director General, All India Radio, or any officer duly authorised by him on his behalf. 'Advertiser' means any individual or organisation including a commercial concern, which has offered an advertisement for broadcast over the radio.

'Advertising Agency' means any organisation, which is accredited to, registered with AIR a such. 'Advertisement' includes any item of publicity for goods or services inserted in the programmes broadcast by the competent authority in consideration of payment to All India Radio. Spot Advertisement means any direct advertisement mentioning product/service, there merit and other related details. The term "Sponsored Programme" means any programme material which is planned, produced and or paid for by an organisation or individual, including a commercial concern to be called "the Sponsor" for the purpose of being broadcast over the Radio.

Scope

The Director General, All India Radio, shall be the sole judge of the suitability or otherwise of an advertisement or a sponsored programme for broadcast his decision in this regard shall be final.

Broadcast time shall be sold to the Advertiser/ Advertising Agencies at the sole discretion of the Director General, All India Radio, according to the prescribed rates. The Advertisement must be clearly distinguishable from the programme. A Sponsored programme shall constitute a substantive broadcast/ programme, as distinct from material which directly advertise any specific wares or goods/products/services. The name of the sponsor shall be broadcast immediately before and after the sponsored programme.

The Sponsor shall, however, undertake to indemnify All India Radio against any legal claim that may be brought against it as a result of the broadcast of a Sponsored Programme or any portion thereof. Advertising is an important and legitimate means for the seller to awaken interest in his goods and services. The success of advertising depends on public confidence; hence no practice should be permitted which tends to impair this confidence. The standards laid down here should be taken as minimum standards of acceptability, which would be liable to be reviewed from time to time in relation to the prevailing norm of listener's susceptibilities.

The following standards of conduct are laid down in order to develop and promote healthy advertising practices in All India Radio. Responsibility for the observance of these rules rests equally upon the Advertiser and the Advertising Agency.

All those engaged in advertising are strongly recommended to familiarise themselves with the legislation affecting advertising in this country, particularly the following Acts and the Rules framed under them:

- Drugs and Cosmetics Act, 1940.
- Drugs Control Act, 1950.
- Drugs and Magic Remedies (Objectionable Advertisement) Act, 1954.
- Copyright Act, 1957.
- Trade and Merchandise Marks Act, 1958.
- Prevention of Food Adulteration Act, 1954.
- Pharmacy Act, 1948.
- Prize Competition Act, 1955.
- Emblems and Names (Prevention of Improper Use) Act, 1950.

- Consumer Protection Act, 1986.
- Indecent Representation of women (Prohibition) Act, 1986.
- AIR/Doordarshan Code.

Code of Ethics for advertisement in India issued by the Advertising Council of India Code of standards in relation to the advertising of medicines and treatments.

General Rules of Conduct in Advertising

Advertising shall be designed as to confirm to the laws of the country and should not offend against morality, decency and religious susceptibilities of the people.

No advertisement shall be permitted which:

- Derides any race, caste, colour, creed and nationality; is against any of the directive principles, or any other provision of the Constitution of India;
- Tends to incite people to crime, cause disorder or violence, or breach of law or glorifies violence or obscenity in any way;
- Presents criminality as desirable;
- Adversely affects friendly relations with foreign States;
- Exploits the national emblem, or any part of the constitution or the person or personality of a national leader or State Dignitary;
- Relates to or promotes cigarettes and tobacco products, liquor, wines and other intoxicants;
- No advertisements message shall in any way be presented as News.
- No advertisements shall be permitted the objects whereof are wholly or mainly of a religious or political natures; advertisement must not be

directed towards any religious or political end or have relation to any industrial dispute.

Advertisements for services concerned with the following shall not be accepted:

— Money lenders.
— Chit funds.
— Saving schemes and lotteries other than those conducted by Centeral and State Government organisations, nationalised or recognised banks and public sector undertakings.
— Matrimonial agencies.
— Unlicenced employment services.
— Fortune tellers or sooth-sayers etc. and those with claims of hypnotism.
— Foreign goods and foreign banks.
— Betting tips and guide books etc. relating to horse-racing or the other games of chance.
— The items advertised shall not suffer from any defect or deficiency as mentioned in Consumer Protection Act 1986.
— No advertisement shall contain reference which are likely to lead the public to infer that the product advertised or any advertised or any of its ingredients has some special or miraculous or super-natural property or quality, which is difficult of being proved, e.g. cure for baldness, skin whitener, etc.
— No advertisement shall contain the words 'Guarantee' or 'Guaranteed' etc., unless the full terms of the guarantee are available for inspection by the Directorate General, All India Radio, are clearly set out in the advertisement and are made available to the purchaser in the writing at the

point of sale or with the goods; in all cases, terms must include details of the remedial action available to the purchaser.

No advertisement shall contain a direct or implied reference to any guarantee, which purports to take away or diminish the legal rights of the purchaser. Advertisers or the agents must be prepared to produce evidence to substantiate any claims or illustrations. The Director General reserves the right to ask for such proofs and get them examined to his full satisfaction. In case of goods covered by mandatory quality control orders, the advertiser shall produce quality certificate from the institutions recognised by the Government for this purpose.

Advertisements shall not contain disparaging of derogatory references to another product or service. Testimonials must be genuine and used in a manner not to mislead the listeners.

Advertisers or Advertising Agencies must be prepared to produce evidence in support of their claims.

No advertisement of any kind of jewellery or precious stones shall be accepted. Information to consumers on matters of weight, quality or prices of products where given shall be accurate.

Advertisements indicating price comparisons or reductions must comply with relevant laws.

No advertisement shall be accepted which violates AIR Broadcast Code which is reproduced below: -

General Air Code

- Criticism of friendly countries.
- Attack of religious or communities.
- Anything obscene or defamatory.

- Incitement to violence or anything against maintenance of law and order.
- Anything amounting to contempt of court.
- Aspersions against the integrity of the President and Judiciary.

Any such effects which might startle the listening public must not be incorporated in advertisements. For example, and without limiting the scope, the use of the following sound effects will not be permitted:

- Rapid gunfire or rifle shots.
- Sirens.
- Bombardments.
- Screams.
- Raucous laughter and the like.

Any pretence in advertising copy must be avoided and such copy shall not be accepted by All India Radio. The 'simulation' of voices of a personality in connection with advertisements for commercial products is also prohibited unless bonafide evidence is available that such personality has given permission for the simulation and it is clearly understood that station broadcasting such announcements are indemnified by the advertiser or advertising agency against any possible legal action.

ADVERTISING AND CHILDREN

No advertising for a product or service shall be accepted if it suggests in any way that unless the children themselves buy or encourage other people to buy the products or services, they will be failing in their duty or lacking in loyalty to any person or organisation.

No advertisement shall be accepted which leads children to believe that if they do not own or use the product advertised they will be inferior in some way to other children or that they are liable to the condemned or ridiculed for not owning or using it.

No advertisement likely to bring advertising into contempt or disrepute shall be permitted. Advertising shall not take advantage of the superstition or ignorance of the general public.

No advertising of talismans, charms and character reading from photographs or such other matter as well as those, which trade on superstition of general public, shall be permitted.

Advertising shall be truthful, avoid distorting facts and misleading the public by means of implications by false statements, as to:

- The character of the merchandise, i.e. its utility, materials, ingredients, origin etc.
- The price of the merchandise, its value, its suitability or terms of purchase.
- The services accompanying purchase, including delivery, exchange, return, repair, upkeep etc.
- Personal recommendations of the article or service the quality or the value of competing goods or trustworthiness of statement made by others.

Testimonials of any kind from experts etc. other than Government recognised standardisation agencies shall not be permitted. No advertisement shall be permitted to contain any claim so exaggerated as to lead inevitably to disappointment in the minds of the public.

Methods of advertising designated to create confusion in the mind of the consumer as between goods by one maker and another maker are unfair and shall not be used. Such methods may consist in:

- The imitation of the trademark of the name of competition or packaging or labelling of goods; or

— The imitation of advertising devices, copy, layout or slogans.

Indecent, vulgar, suggestive, repulsive or offensive themes or treatment shall be avoided in all advertisements. This also supplies to such advertisements which themselves are not objectionable as defined above, but which advertise objectionable books, photographs or other matter and thereby lead to their sale and circulation.

4

DIRECT MAIL ADVERTISING

Advertising mail, also known as, Direct mail, junk mail, or admail, is the delivery of advertising material to recipients of postal mail. The delivery of advertising mail forms a large and growing service for many postal services, and direct mail marketing forms a significant portion of the direct marketing industry. Some organisations attempt to help people opt-out of receiving advertising mail, in many cases motivated by a concern over its negative environmental impact.

Advertising mail includes advertising circulars, catalogs, CDs, "pre-approved" credit card applications, and other commercial merchandising materials delivered to both homes and businesses. It may be addressed to pre-selected individuals, or unaddressed and delivered on a neighbourhood-by-neighbourhood basis.

Direct mail is everywhere. One of the least expensive ways to participate in a direct-mail campaign is to team up with other businesses in a cooperative effort—Valpak and Carol Wright envelopes are great examples of that. With this approach, you're able to choose specific ZIP codes to be covered, giving you the ability to control your costs. You also have a say in how your ads or coupons are printed—single or double-sided, two- or four-colour, glossy or matte paper—giving you further control. With this particular type of direct mail, however, your piece is just one of 30 or 40 others in the envelope. So you have to make sure your printed piece will catch the eye of the person who's flipping through all those ads, And because these envelopes blanket an entire ZIP code, reaching all the included addresses—businesses as well as residential—you have to understand that not all the destinations will be ones you'd hand pick.

When you contact these cooperative companies, be sure to ask about their mailing schedules. They won't target all ZIP codes every month—there are specific times of year when you can mail to the areas you want. So get those dates and deadlines—the company will be happy to give you the entire year's schedule so you can make your plans.

You can also choose to send out individual direct-mail pieces—meaning you aren't sharing space with others—by having them designed, printed and mailed by a mail house or direct mail company. These firms have the ability to specifically target the recipients of your ads, not only by geographic area but also by the habits, hobbies, talents, schooling and reading preferences of your customers, among other things. While this kind of direct mail costs more than a cooperative effort, a much higher percentage of your ads will be getting into qualified hands—that is, into the hands of a larger number of your target customers. Also, with this type of mailing, you're not bound by any predetermined mailing schedule. But be aware of the fixed costs that these companies have no control over:

- Postage.
- Paper.
- How elaborate your direct mail piece is in terms of design and colours.
- Size (postcard-size to large, foldout pieces).

Direct mail pieces also show up in your Sunday newspaper every week. They're called "inserts" and can be parceled out to the ZIP codes of your choice. How does it work? You assume the cost of printing the inserts and the responsibility for delivering the ads to the newspaper or publication by a specific deadline.

Did you know that many distributors will supply insert ads at no charge to you (with the possible exception of the cost of shipping them to you), and some will even have the ads pre-printed with your business name and location to help you promote their brands? Check with all your manufacturers and distributors to see what's available. Often, these pre-printed ads are more readily available around certain holidays, but sometimes the companies provide them all year long.

If you're interested in reaching businesses rather than homes, contact the chambers of commerce in the areas you want to reach. Often, if you provide the coupons or ads, they'll insert them into one of their monthly mailings for a nominal fee, which is often less than Rs. 5,000.

To help determine the most important ZIP codes to hit, keep track of your customers. Ask them for their ZIP code when they make a purchase. It's not unusual; you've probably been asked for yours over and over again. Do what those other stores are doing, and keep track of where the people who shop at your location live. Make sure all of your employees ask each customer as they process the sale and make sure they write the information down. Once you start doing that, you'll see a pattern and can tell where, other than your own neighborhood, you should be sending direct mail in the form of ads or coupons.

Direct-mail pieces can be sent right along with your monthly invoices, too. Stuff an ad into each envelope—in fact, this is a great place for a coupon since these people are already your customers and don't need to be totally educated about your business. A coupon will be a little "gift" for them to use the next time they do business with you.

ADVANTAGES OF DIRECT MAIL ADVERTISING

Direct mail encompasses a wide variety of marketing materials, including brochures, catalogs, postcards, newsletters and sales letters. Major corporations already know direct-mail advertising is one of the most effective and profitable ways to reach out to new and existing clients.

Unlike other forms of advertising, in which you're never sure just who is getting your message, direct mail lets you communicate one-on-one with your target audience. That allows you to control who receives your message, when it is delivered, what is in the envelope, and how many people you reach.

To create an effective direct-mail campaign, start by getting your name on as many mailing lists as possible. Junk mail isn't junk when you're trying to learn about direct mail. Obtain free information every chance you get, especially from companies that offer products or services similar to yours. Take note of your reaction to each piece of mail, and save the ones that communicate most effectively, whether they come from large or small companies.

The most effective direct-mail inserts often use key words, colours and formats that can be adapted into your own mailer. Make sure the colours you use promote the appropriate image. Neon colours, for example, can attract attention for party planner or gift basket businesses. On the other hand, ivory and gray are usually the colours of choice for lawyers, financial planners and other business services.

To involve the reader in the ordering process, many mailers enclose stickers that say Yes or No to be pasted on the order form. Companies such as Publishers' Clearinghouse take this technique further by asking recipients to find hidden stickers throughout the mailing and paste them on the sweepstakes entry. It also asks customers to choose their prizes, which gets them even more involved.

POSTAL SERVICES

Postal systems have enacted lower rates for buyers of bulk mail permits. In order to qualify for these rates, marketers must format and sort the mail in specific ways—which reduces the handling required by the postal service.

Income from advertising mail represents a significant and growing portion of some postal service's budgets, and it is a service actively marketed by them. In Canada, addressed and unaddressed advertising mail accounted for 20% of Canada Post's revenue in 2005, and the share is increasing. Postal services employ the terms advertising mail, admail, and direct mail, while avoiding and objecting to the pejorative term junk mail. In many developed countries, advertising mail represents a significant and growing amount of the total volume of mail.

DIRECT MAIL MARKETING

Design and Format

Direct mail permits the marketer to design marketing pieces in many different formats. Indeed, there is an entire subsector of the industry that produces specialised papers, printing, envelopes, and other materials for direct mail marketing. Some of the common formats include:

— *Catalogues:* Multi-page, bound promotions, usually featuring a selection of products for sale.

— *Self-mailers:* Pieces usually created from a single sheet that has been printed and folded. For instance, a common practice is to print a page-length advertisement or promotion on one side of a sheet of paper. This is then folded in half or in thirds, with the promotional message to the inside. The two outside surfaces are then used for the address of the recipient and some "teaser" message designed to persuade the customer to open the piece.

— *Clear bag packages:* Large (often 9x12 or bigger) full-colour packages sealed in a clear, plastic outer wrap. The contents show through the clear bag, giving the potential for maximum initial impact. Clear bag packages can be extremely effective and are very affordable based upon the campaign open-rate.

— *Postcards:* Simple, two-sided pieces, with a promotional message on one side and the customer's address on the other.

— *Envelope mailers*: Mailings in which the marketing material is placed inside an envelope. This permits the marketer to include more than one insert. When more than one advertiser is included, this is often called "marriage mail".

— *Snap mailers:* Mailers that fold and seal with pressure. The sides detach and the mailer is opened to reveal the message.

— *Dimensional mailers:* Mailers that have some dimension to them, like a small box.

— *Intelligent documents:* Programmable mail pieces built dynamically from database information, and printed digitally for faster production.

Advantages and Disadvantages

Many people respond positively to direct mail advertising and find useful goods and services on offer. Traditionally, this was more true in rural areas where people had to travel many miles to do their shopping and direct mail and mail order shopping was a major convenience. However, some people dislike it, in the same way as with' calls and, as noted above, e-mail spam, and some jurisdictions like the US have laws requiring junk mailers to withhold their offerings from residents who opt out.

Advantages for marketers include the following:

— *Targeting:* Historically, the most important aspect of direct mail was its ability to precisely target previous customers. If a suitable list was available, it could do a good job of targeting prospects.

— *Personalisation:* Direct mail can address the customer personally and be tailored to their needs based on previous transactions and gathered data.

— *Optimisation:* Because of its direct accountability, direct mail can be tested to find the best list; the best offer; the best timing. Then the winning tests can be rolled out to a wider audience for optimal results.

— *Analysis:* The bulk mailing is large enough to allow statistical analyses. For example the results can be analysed to see in detail the performance of individual offers in say a squinch report which shows sales per square inch. With suitable media or source codes, the performance of lists can be captured. These enable better selection of offers and lists for future mailings.

— *Accumulation:* Responses can be added to the database, allowing future mailings to be better targeted.

Advocates make the following arguments.

— Efficient use of advertising fund.

— Highly selective, targeted and personalised.

— Flexible.

— High quality reproduction.

— Response easily measured.

Disadvantages include

— *Cost*: The cost per thousand will be higher than almost any other form of mass promotion (although the wastage rate may be much lower). Also, development costs in database acquisition/ development. It is however important to note that despite the production and development costs, direct mail can be very profitable, if executed correctly. Lastly, when comparing different media costs, return on investment is the best measure.

— *Waste:* Large quantities of paper and plastic are thrown away.

— *Alienation*: Some recipients resent direct marketing being "forced" upon them, and boycott companies that do so. Moreover, they may obtain Prohibitory Orders against companies whose direct marketing mail they find offensive.

Targeting

Advertisers often call direct mail "targeted mailing", since mail is usually sent out following database analysis. For example a person who purchases golf supplies may receive direct mail for golf related products or perhaps for goods and services that are appropriate for golfers. When direct mail uses database analysis, it is a type of database marketing.

Advances in computing and communications technology have significantly impacted the direct mailing industry in recent years. As computers become more powerful and databases become larger, new opportunities arise for direct mail companies to perform more in-depth processing of their mailing lists. Mailings can be targeted based on location and demographic data. This allows mailings to be targeted more specifically and potentially increases response rates. Web sites are appearing which allow clients to create their mailing lists interactively using map-based interfaces.

Personalised Uniform Resource Locator (URLs)

Personalised URLs, also known as PURLs, are personalised websites used in conjunction with direct mail that are designed to gather information about the person that visits it. Marketing companies find this useful when testing marketing methods and response rates.

Personalised URLs are generally printed on the direct mail piece in the format JohnSample.domain.com or domain.com/JohnSample. They recognise the individual who is visiting the site and can welcome them by name. They also have the ability to obtain and disperse detailed and specific information pertaining to the individual looking at the site.

Personalised URLs are assigned to individual recipients based on the direct mail campaign database and are included either as the only variable or as one of several variable fields in the larger variable data printing communication. When recipients of the direct mail piece log onto their PURL, the information from the campaign database is used to tailor the web page experience to that specific recipient. They are referenced by name, and the graphics, text, offers, and other information on the page can also be tailored to them personally, based on the information in the marketer's database.Studies have shown that people prefer to get additional information online, so Personalised URLs create a seamless way to connect the printed piece to the Web.

Business-to-Business Mailings (B2B)

Business products and services have long used direct mail to promote themselves. Traditionally, this worked in one of two ways. As a direct sale, therefore precluding the use of a salesperson or a retail store, or as a method of generating leads for a salesforce. The former method was ideally used by products that were easy to sell, were familiar to the prospect and needed no demonstration. The latter method was used for large ticket items or for those that needed demonstration for example.

Opting out

In some other countries, several organisations offer opt-out services to people who wish to reduce or eliminate the amount of addressed advertising mail they receive. In the United Kingdom, the Mailing Preference Service allows people to register with them for removal from posted as opposed to hand delivered mail. In the United States, the Direct Marketing Association's Mail Preference Service functions similar to telemarketing do not call registries, though mailer participation in voluntary.

In Canada, the highly-publicised Red Dot Campaign offers advice on reducing unaddressed advertising mail. The campaign focuses on advertising the Canada Post policy to respect "No Junkmail" signs, noting that this policy is not promoted by Canada Post itself. The name "red dot" refers to an internal marker used by Canada Post to indicate which households do not wish to receive unaddressed admail. The UK Royal Mail also offers an opt-out service, though it sparked public outrage by warning that unaddressed government mailings could not be separated from advertisements, and those who opted-out of the latter would stop receiving the former as well.

Writing Subheads for Direct Mail

The importance of writing subheads for direct mail and online sales letters is often overlooked. Writing a solid subhead begins with a few ground rules to make every sales letter effective.

— *Sales letters for direct mail*: When was the last time you received an uninspiring sales letter that was a front and back page of text, text, text? No bold. No italics. No imagination. Just gobs of information on white paper. With sales letters, subheads can be the key to turning a scanner into a potential customer. Use subheads in your sales letter to break up the sections of your copy.

You can be creative with your subheads for a sales letter. You want to make sure that your subhead isn't too cutesy. You have some flexibility here over writing an online sales letter but your number one goal is to write a subhead that entices that prospect to keep on reading. Your subhead needs to tell your readers why they must read that section. Otherwise, they'll keep skimming and never read the body of your sales letter.

— *Online sales letters* : When you publish a sales letter online, you need to change subheads that you used for direct mail. Online sales letters need subheads that will bring in additional traffic because you used Search Engine Optimisation (SEO) to create them. You don't want your subhead to be so clever that search engines skip over it. You'll lose more customers that way because search engines won't pick up the keywords you could have used to make your subhead effective for the reader and search engines.

5

ADVERTISING ON TV CHANNELS

The vast majority of television advertisements today consist of brief advertising spots, ranging in length from a few seconds to several minutes. Advertisements of this sort have been used to sell every product imaginable over the years, from household products to goods and services, to political campaigns. The effect of television advertisements upon the viewing public has been so successful and so pervasive that it is considered impossible for a politician to wage a successful election campaign, in the United States, without use of television advertising. In certain countries, such as in India and France, political advertisement is strictly limited on television.

Many television advertisements feature catchy jingles or catch-phrases that generate sustained appeal, which may remain in the minds of television viewers long after the span of the advertising campaign. Some of these ad jingles or catch-phrases may take on lives of their own, spawning gags or "riffs" that may appear in other forms of media, such as comedy movies or television variety shows, or in written media, such as magazine comics or literature. These long-lasting advertising elements may therefore be said to have taken a place in the pop culture history of the demographic to which they have appeared.

Advertising agencies often use humour as a tool in their creative marketing campaigns. In fact, many psychological studies tried to demonstrate the effect of humour and indicate the way to empower advertising persuasion. Animation is often used in advertisements. The pictures can vary from hand-drawn traditional animation to computer animation. By using animated characters, an advertisement may have a certain appeal that is difficult to achieve with actors or mere product displays. For this reason, an animated advertisement can be very long-running, several decades in many instances.

TELEVISION ADVERTISING: PROS AND CONS

On average, the general population spends over four and a half hours a day in front of the tube, making TV watching one of the most common modern leisure activities. Is it any wonder then that television advertising is also the most powerful form of advertising? Advertising on television allows you to show and tell a wide audience your business, product, or service. It allows you to actually demonstrate the benefits of ownership. You can show how your product or service works and how it's packaged so prospective customers will know what to look for at the point of sale. In advertising, it often takes multiple touch points to effectively influence consumers' purchasing behaviour.

Television advertising has been a popular medium for large retailers ever since the TV first began to appear in living rooms. With the arrival of cable television came lowered production costs and the opportunity to reach smaller, more targeted markets, making it a viable option for small to medium-size businesses as well. To create an effective television ad, it's first necessary to have a good script that highlights a strong offer. Ads must also be effectively produced, and it's for this reason that it's often better to enlist the services of an advertising agency, which can help you create an entire campaign.

Some of the advantages to advertising your small business on television include the following:

- TV reaches a much larger audience than local newspapers and radio stations, and it does so during a short period of time.
- It reaches viewers when they're the most attentive.
- It allows you to convey your message with sight, sound, and motion, which can give your business, product, or service instant credibility.
- It gives you an opportunity to be creative and attach a personality to your business, which can be particularly effective for small businesses that rely on repeat customers.

ADVANTAGES OF TELEVISION ADVERTISING

With all the kinds of businesses springing up everywhere, competition is very tough and you need to put to use all techniques to have an edge against your competitors. In these modern times, advertising by TV Ad space is one sure way to attract a wider audience than other means of advertising.

As almost every household owns a television and majority of the people are spending more time in front of the television, companies are finding it profitable to invest in advertising by TV Ad space. Finding that it yields greater returns and results than other forms of advertising, companies are considering this method of advertising as a necessary business expense. People watch news, entertainment, films, and other programmes on television and promoting your products on popular shows reaches out to a wider audience. Home viewers don't want to be left behind by what's the latest fad or fashion. They would want to buy the latest products that they see on television. This is because the mass media plays a great influence on people's choices nowadays.

If you think that you have to shell out huge amounts from your savings when you go for advertising by TV Ad space, you are wrong. You don't have to be a corporate giant to be able to do it. Even small companies can create their own advertisement on television to fit within their budget. Whether you spend lakhs of rupees or just a few hundred rupees for advertising on television can give you the same benefit because you get the same target audience. You can also hire the services of freelance advertisers and student interns to save on your budget.

Local cable operators in your area could provide you with another way of saving or lessening your expenses in television advertising. Usually, local cable operators have TV ad spaces which advertisers can avail of at a considerably lower price than the rates set by national television stations. You can also consult an expert when you are planning to create your TV ad campaign. Experts can help you maximise the space you will rent for your TV ad and make it worth every cent of your budget. Go for clear and convincing advertisements because this can bring in more benefits for your company.

Try to stretch your budget so you could avail of placing your advertisements by television especially during the prime time, although these spaces could be more expensive. During prime time, the members of the family are usually present and the more exposure your product gets, the more sales you can generate.

Do not be discouraged if your company is not that big because company size is not a hindrance in TV advertising. You can be creative about it to make it fit around your budget yet at the same time you can maximise your exposure to your targeted audience and expand your potential profits. The rates for advertising by TV Ad space increases with the inevitable increase in the price of other commodities. Start expanding your exposure by TV Ad space now and reap the results sooner.

Some advantages of television advertising include the following:

— Television reaches very large audiences—usually much larger than the audience your local newspaper reaches, and it does so during a short period of time.

— Since there are fewer television stations than radio stations in a given area, each TV audience is divided into much larger segments, which enables you to reach a larger, yet, more diverse audience.

— It has the ability to convey your message with sight, sound and motion, and can give a product or service instant validity and prominence.

— You can easily reach targeted audiences. Children can be reached during cartoon programming, housewives during the afternoon soap operas, and insomniacs after midnight.

DISADVANTAGES OF TELEVISION ADVERTISING

— When you advertise on TV, your commercial is not only competing with others, it is also competing with the viewer's environment as well.

— Even if your commercial is being aired, viewers may never see it unless it is intrusive enough to capture their attention.

— A minimum amount of airtime provides limited length of exposure and ad clutter.

— The message comes and goes, and that's it! Unless you buy additional time, the viewer doesn't see your commercial again.

— Multiple exposures are required to achieve message retention and consumer action. If you don't reach your viewer at least 5-7 times, you are just throwing money away.

— No station loyalty; Viewers have little or no loyalty to the station itself—especially since cable can bring dozens of viewing alternatives into the home. For example, viewers will watch a given channel for a programme they know will be aired at a specific time. If a Cricket match, popular movie or some other preferred form of entertainment appears on another channel, the viewer will not hesitate to switch channels without leaving the couch.

— During a commercial break the viewer may choose to get a snack, go to the bathroom or have a conversation about whatever they were just watching.

— Because of a larger "area of dominant influence," the relative cost will be higher—both the terms of airtime and production.

The "glitz and glamour" associated with producing a television commercial makes it one of the most appealing advertising methods. Carefully consider your budget and other options, however, to be sure a TV ad makes sense for your company.

TOWARDS AN EFFECTIVE TV COMMERCIAL

Put People in Your Commercial

People relate to other people. Putting people into your commercial can help draw your target audience in as opposed to a 30 second shot of your building's interior, exterior and the parking lot. You don't want your commercial to look hokey so you do want to be careful about having people waving at the camera or standing there smiling. Have them doing something that relates to your business so your commercial doesn't look like a photo that's come to life.

Plan Out your Video

Using a furniture store as an example, you may have ten different kinds of recliners, eight living room sets and six bedroom suits you want to feature. You're going to have to narrow those shots down because you simply can't get them all into a :30, :45 or even a one minute commercial without flashing so many different pieces of video on the screen that your potential customers will feel like they're in a lightning storm. Wide shots of your showroom are good to get a bunch of your furniture displayed at once and you can select a few items you want to be featured alone. It's crucial you not cram a bunch of video into the small amount of time you have for your commercial. Your video should tell the story about what you're advertising even if a customer has their volume turned down.

Writing the Script

Make sure your commercial's script times out to 30 seconds. Use short sentences that grab your potential customer's attention. You've got a very limited time frame to capture your audience and you need to get your message across quickly. Don't get wrapped up in long sentences. Keep them short and punchy. Your audio should also tell the customer what you're advertising even if the customer is in another room and can't see the TV when your commercial airs.

Audio and Video Must Match

When writing your commercial, you must make sure your audio and video match. When you're talking about new car models arriving, you don't want to see video of the current year's make. When you're talking about your big showroom of furniture, you don't want to see the building from the street. You must merge your audio and video to create a powerful sales tool.

Never Forget your Call to Action

Your call to action gets customers to buy or act now. Don't get to the end of your commercial and leave off your call to action. You want to tell customers to visit today and give your complete contact information, including Web site address, phone number and street address (giving a quick line about how to find you if possible). For example, "That's Simple Designs, located next to the old train depot downtown."

Stick to Time

You've bought a 30 seconds commercial package. As tempting as it might be to squeak in an extra few seconds, you just can't do it. Your commercial must time out to the exact time you've paid for. Going over will only get your all-to-important call to action clipped because those last few seconds will be cut off when your commercial airs.

Hiring a Production Company

Of course, you want your commercial to be professional. You can hire a production company or many television stations have their own production companies in-house. They can handle all aspects of your commercial, including writing, shooting and editing your commercial. Shop around for prices. Some production companies are able to offer you a commercial package for as low as Rs. 5,000 that will include still pictures shot with a high quality video camera.

Scheduling your Commercial

Placement of your commercial is very important. It determines who will see your commercial and how much you will pay for its air time. Having your commercial air at 3 a.m. will save your money but if you don't reach your audience it's not money well spent. The same holds true for the station you're airing your ad on as well. If you're advertising your maternity clothing store, you don't want schedule air time on ESPN with your local cable company.

Frequency

Television is less demanding on frequency than radio but it still deserves more than a one-shot deal. If you were advertising during the Indian Idol, that would be a completely different story. But on the local level, you need to identify the key times your ad should run and buy enough air time for your commercial to reach your audience at least twice. More times would be ideal.

Consistency

Use the same announcer, jingle, fonts, colours, etc. to keep your commercial consistent. This helps people start to get to know your company by all of these factors. The more you recognise the lady pitching the hair salon down the street, the more you know exactly what that company's name and address is before she even speaks in the commercial.

You see other businesses and professional services advertising on TV and you think, "They must be making money or they wouldn't keep doing it! Can I make money advertising on TV?"

Well, maybe you can! Many people do! If you have a good offer for TV and a well-crafted commercial placed in the right kind of programming, it can make your phones ring right off the wall.

But everything starts with your offer! If you want immediate phone calls, you must have an offer that is right for what I call "Immediate Response TV". Not everyone does. If you don't, then you may have to depend on longer-term "image" TV advertising or maybe some other kind of advertising altogether.

Let's define our terms: "Image" or "Brand" advertising is what you see mostly on national TV. The main idea is make you feel good about the product or service. Image commercials are really a kind of propaganda. They are usually more expensive to make and can take a long time to work, if they do.

On the other hand, "Immediate Response" advertising attempts to get you to take some buying action right now, such as call the advertiser. Since the small business or professional advertiser usually does not have the time or budget to wait for image ads to work, I specialise in producing immediate response TV commercials for these clients.

6

ADVERTISING ON RADIO

Many traditional businesses cut their advertising budgets during economic downturns, which results in a reduction in demand and a corresponding fall in pricing power by the radio industry. This is an opportunity for direct response radio advertisers because more inventory and lower rates help make for huge profits.

CREATING GREAT RADIO ADS

Profitable direct response radio campaigns are a product of excellent strategy, skilful media buying, and insightful radio commercial development. Here are the top ten keys to creating great radio ads:

Production Value and Voiceover Talent

Contrary to popular belief, these are not the most important element in great ads. Yet they are what clients often use to determine whether they "like" an ad. From the data we've collected through ten years of testing radio ads we've found that there is very often an inverse relationship between production value and ad performance. Yes, that's counterintuitive. Production value shouldn't "hurt" response, right? There are a number of possibilities for why this is true. Maybe good production value distracts ad developers from the right amount of focus on great copywriting. Or, perhaps good production value creates an ad that is so "slick" that it doesn't stand out. As Seth Godin puts it "perfect is boring".

Nonetheless, production and voice are still important. Production must enhance believability, catch attention, and ensure the message can be ingested by the audience with minimal effort. And the voice talent's read must be evaluated for it's non-verbal communication, not just what the words mean as they're strung together.

Distinctiveness of the Offering

The greater the "me too" factor, the lower the potential for the campaign. If your product is another of the hundreds of weight loss products or diets, then you're likely going to have a difficult time coming up with something new to say to people. Distinctiveness applies not just to the product benefits, but also to the creative approach, the offer, and any other element of the campaign.

Effective use of the Interplay between Emotion and Logic

There are points in the ad where emotional appeals are appropriate, and there are other points in the ad where logical appeals are potent. Few people make a purchase decision based solely on one or the other. Quite often we're "reeled in" with emotion, and just before we buy we look for a logical reason to rationalise our emotional decision. Successful radio ads recognise this dynamic and flow accordingly.

Articulation

There are a number of different ways to express your message. Any one can get the message across. But only one is the optimum formula that presents the combination to the lock on the door of your customers' minds. Changing just one word or a few words in an ad can have an amazingly large impact on results. We've seen this over and over again—some key insight that produces a small copy change that dramatically boosts results. Or the opposite. Articulation matters. One of the biggest mistakes we've seen is using wishy-washy, non-specific language. Saying something "Product A is designed to do X" is not as strong as saying "Product A does X".

Simplicity

You have sixty seconds. Packing too much into the ad overwhelms the listener, triggering the natural cognitive processes that minimise sensory overload. Leave the kitchen sink in the kitchen. If the kitchen sink is what's so impressive about your product or service, then at least test a focused approach next to it so you can learn which performs better.

Use of Sound Elements to Enhance the Message

This is radio. The theatre of the mind. In TV you can just show someone. In radio, you show them with sound. It's both a burden and a benefit of radio advertising because it's both harder to do but more impactful when done well.

Authenticity

This is hard to do because we're so conditioned to look outside our business for clues as to how to succeed. The result is inauthenticity. Me-too-ism. All things to nobody or nothing to everybody. The best radio ads flow from an authentic connection to a product or service's uniqueness, passion, and identity. Authenticity is influential, believable and enhances credibility. It is also a differentiator (unfortunately).

The Offer

As with nearly any direct response advertisement, there must be a call to action that is relevant, compelling and simple enough to grasp quickly. Relevant means it matters to a potential customer—it reduces my risk, makes picking up the phone a no-brainer, or gives me a reason to go with my emotions instead of my logic. Compelling means it has a "wow" factor. As in, "wow, they must really believe in their product to do that. And simple means it's... not complicated. It doesn't make me stop and think too much. It doesn't confuse me with language that's spun to sound like it's a great offer but really isn't. One insight is pivotal here: the business model must be built with the potential offers in mind. Think about it—you can't make an offer in an ad that you can't afford to make.

The Opening Attention Grabber

The first impression of a great radio ad must provoke a desire for further exploration. If not, the radio ad will be categorised by the brain as the same old noise it always hears. And it will be blocked out—a victim of the cognitive processes that ensure we don't experience sensory overload. The challenge of grabbing attention is huge. Don't underestimate it. This is a difficult thing to do. Why? Because we're all bombarded relentlessly by huge number of other advertisers who are trying to do it.

One way to think about this is 'don't bury the lead'. Make sure that the most impactful aspect of your ad is expressed early on. Don't wait until 20 seconds into the ad to make your first point.

Benefit Orientation

One of the biggest mistakes made is assuming people care how something works before they care what it does for them. You must only say how if the what is so incredible that you need a "reason to believe" in the ad—and then you do it in one sentence or less. Clients seem to love the how, but it typically doesn't sell.

The ad must answer the question: what's in it for me? How will it impact my life in a way that I think it will make my life better, happier, or easier? This requires understanding and tapping into the fundamental human beliefs around these topics. A product that prevents a problem I don't yet have? I don't care about that because I have current problems that matter more to me. Prevention doesn't sell. What does sell is something that solves my problem quickly, safely, better and more conveniently than anything else. If you use your 60 seconds in any other way, you're wasting time.

DIRECT RESPONSE RADIO ADVERTISING

Direct response radio advertising is an amazingly under recognised way to grow a business quickly and profitably. For one thing, it's fully accountable, so every dollar spent can be tracked to the revenue it generates and unprofitable spending can be eliminated. In addition, it's extremely scalable. Once you figure out what works, you can increase your revenues and profits simply by increasing your media spend. It's nearly as easy as stepping on the gas pedal. Direct response radio advertising is truly a powerful engine for profitable growth.

When it is done properly. Most of the time, radio advertising is not done right. The first step in "doing radio right" is not to do it until you're ready. The questions will help you determine whether you're ready to take advantage of direct response radio advertising.

Do You Know How You Will Define Success?

How much, in profit, is each customer worth to your

business over the course of that customer's relationship with your company? This is the customer lifetime value question and it is vital to know this before you go into direct response advertising. Why? Because the definition of success in direct response radio advertising is acquiring a new customer at a cost that allows for a profitable relationship with that new customer. If you don't know the lifetime value, you cannot know how much you are able to pay to acquire a customer.

Think about the day when you run your first ad schedule on a station. The results come in. How do you know whether they are good or bad? Are they good because there is revenue? Are they good because the phone is ringing or because visits to the web site went up? These are not sufficient to understand and evaluate the performance of your advertising. You can only evaluate advertising performance within the context of your customer lifetime value.

But knowing your customer lifetime value is not enough. You have to break this down into the metrics that you'll use to evaluate and manage your campaign. These metrics are part of the formula for lifetime value, metrics like "cost per lead" (CPL), cost per order (CPO), also known as CPA or (cost per acquisition), conversion rate, and average revenue per sale. Do not begin a direct response radio advertising campaign (or a business of any sort using any kind of demand generation tactics) until you know your business profitability metrics very well.

Are You Prepared to Test?

We have often heard people say "We tried radio advertising and it doesn't work for us".

Here's the problem with that statement: Developing a profitable direct response radio advertising campaign isn't something that is accomplished with a "trial". It is far too complicated an endeavour, with far too many variables, to assess its effectiveness for your business with a "trial". There are creative variables and media variables, and together they present a daunting number of possible combinations to achieve success.

To properly assess the potential for direct response radio advertising to generate profitable new customers for your business, you must approach direct response radio advertising with a testing mindset. That calls for a patient, methodical approach.

What does this mean for you? It means that you need around Rs. 1,000,000 to test multiple ads over a 4-8 week period before you'll know which approaches will (and won't) yield more profitable results. Don't go into direct response radio advertising with a "dabble" mindset. Go into it with solid business goals: *(a)* To assess the potential of direct response radio advertising to drive profitable new revenues, and *(b)* to understand which approaches—both creative and media—produce the best results for your company. While you'll generate revenues and profits during the test, the real benefit of testing is in the learnings that can be applied to a larger campaign over a long period of time to drive significant sales and profits.

Do You have a Compelling Offer?

The offer in your direct response radio ad is one of the most important elements for success. But why do you need to be thinking about that before you even approach radio advertising? Isn't that something your radio advertising agency should come up with? Well, yes, but... The "but" here hinges on the fact that any offer must be something that's possible given the business profitability structure, and possible given the systems and processes that run the business. These are constraints that only you know about. It will take time to alter existing systems or processes should that be necessary to support a compelling offer in your advertising. Your agency might recommend you give away a free DVD player with each order. That would drive a lot of orders, but would they be profitable? You need to define the playing field for the agency and then engage in the dialogue of getting the most out of what's possible given the constraints.

What is a compelling offer? It's different, it's relevant, and it's meaningful. A free complimentary product or service is a good example. For example, if you're marketing a skin care product that fights acne, you can give away a skin softener product as a bonus. Others use free trials with conversion mechanisms. These can work well provided the product performs as promised. Still others employ the 'risk free trial' approach, which essentially positions the 30 day money back guarantee as an offer—a "risk free trial". The possibilities are many.

Is your Business Infrastructure set up to Support Direct Response Advertising?

The most important aspect of preparing for direct response radio advertising is ensuring you're ready for the volume of leads and orders that can result. The easiest way to project this is to know your CPL and CPO projections and then assume a specific weekly media spend. For example, say you're running Rs. 1,250,000 in media per week in direct response radio. This is considered a relatively small campaign. If your business model shows that you expect a CPL of Rs. 750, then you'll be driving 1,250,000/750 = 1666 calls per week. Can your sales call center and fulfillment center handle this volume? More importantly, can they handle more, because when you're profitable while running a Rs. 1,250,000 weekly radio campaign, you'll undoubtedly want to grow to five to ten times that size as soon as possible.

There's another vital piece of infrastructure you absolutely must have in place before you begin direct response radio advertising. It is a firm requirement because without it you're wasting your money and ruining your reputation with the vendors you've hired to help you build the campaign. That requirement is excellent data collection and transmission to the radio media buying department at your radio agency. By this we mean that you absolutely must have a mechanism for capturing the lead, order, and revenue data by the unique identifier for the media buy that generated the call. If you're sending calls to a call center, this is no problem. They understand this need and are already set up to accommodate it. If you're trying to take calls in house, most of the time you've got work to do to ensure you can provide your media company with the information they need on a timely basis. If you are sending leads to a web site, which is happening with increasing frequency, you must set up data capture and transmission mechanisms via a web tracking software program like Google Analytics before the campaign begins, preferably before you even contact a direct response radio advertising agency to get started. It's amazing how many times we've been told that this tracking mechanism is in place and that we'll get daily data exports from the web tracking software, only to begin the test and find out we won't be receiving data for many days and what we do receive will not be complete.

Are you Aware of Your Biases and Assumptions?

This question probably sounds a little different than the rest but it's well worth spending some time on. What you must understand is that you, the client, lead the show. As the agency, we will tell you want we recommend based on our expertise in the field of direct response radio advertising. It's up to you to make sure we're making those recommendations with all of the necessary information. Biases and assumptions can damage this important aspect of the client-agency relationship.

Biases and assumptions underlie beliefs you have about key campaign questions like why your customers buy from you, or what appeals in advertising will resonate with the target audience. If you inject these into the process as facts, your agency will likely take them as such. The agency is unlikely to argue strongly with you—- it's just the nature of the "the customer is always right" tendency in client-agency relationships.

Let's say you've been advertising online with banners and pay per click. You want to test radio. One common mistake is to do a survey of your existing customers and ask them why they buy. The results show that the reasons these people buy match up very well with the appeals in the advertisements that you've been running. You conclude that the exact same approach will work in radio and you require that approach be followed by the agency. But you've overlooked the fact that your survey was very biased. Why? Because the people you surveyed were prompted to become customers by the ads you ran. Of course you're going to find people who validate the ads you've run—they responded to them to become customers! The non-biased way to do a survey is to collect data from a random sample of people matching the target customer profile.

Notice the point is not to eradicate your biases or assumptions, but to become aware of them. It's nearly impossible to get rid of biases. However, if you're aware of them you can then test them methodically and you won't be in danger of leading your agency down the wrong path—one that often leads to the failure of radio campaigns.

Are you Different?

Me-too products or services don't work, period. In direct response you find this out quickly. You must be different. One important twist to this is that you can be different in any one of a number of different ways. As a certain marketing professor liked to say "you can innovate anywhere in the value chain...the more places the better". Did Dell Computer make innovative new computers? Not at all. Dell found a way to put computers together faster, with higher reliability and at a lower cost than any other PC maker. That, among other things, translated into a super low cost structure which meant Dell could beat competitors on price and still make more money than those competitors. There are other examples. Maybe you're marketing a product in the diet aid category. There are "support" food programmes, pills and informational/diet regimens. Do you have to have the latest breakthrough pill to compete? That would be nice but there are only so many of those to be discovered. So you can be different in another way. Your spokesperson could be a celebrity. Your marketing angle could be radically different. Your offer could be unique. Your cost structure or overall business model might allow for an incredible free gift or a very low price. Your customer retention programme might be so strong that you can give away a free trial to acquire large numbers of customers. There are many, many ways to be different. How you're different—while important—is still second to the fact that if you're a me-too product you'll not last long.

ADVERTISING STRATEGY AND CREATIVE DEVELOPMENT

The first part is the advertising strategy and creative development of your radio ads. These get lumped together because to charge off creating a radio ad before conducting a basic strategy exercise is a big mistake and a total waste of time and money. That's the fire-aim-ready approach.

Thanks to technological advances, the costs of radio ad development have come down dramatically over the last decade. A good ballpark range for a single-voice radio ad is Rs. 42,500-Rs.45,000. This includes creative strategy, copywriting and production. For additional voices, figure in another Rs.7500-Rs.10000. It's not necessary to ever pay more than Rs.50,000 for a radio ad unless you have an unusually complex production requirement, like many different voices or special studio requirements—or, if a lot of copy changes are made and significant re-voicing and re-editing is required.

Budget the cost to create two spots to test. The one that performs the best becomes the control ad. At this point refine both the ad and the media elements to maximise the performance of the ad. If neither of the first two ads performs above your break-even level, more tests of copy and the presentation of different appeals are needed to produce that outcome.

You want the proper incentives in place to align your interests with your agency's interests so you get the best creative strategy, the best copywriting, and the right voices and production. This is not the place to pinch pennies. If you have budget constraints, discuss them with your agency because if the strategy and creative process fails, the rest of the campaign will fail.

Media Planning and Media Buying

The second component of radio costs is the media budget. The media budget has two phases. Phase one is the weekly testing budget spent early in the campaign which focuses in on the strategy, creative and media variables that result in maximum profitability. When we do a test, we establish a weekly test budget over a four week period. Typically, the budget is around Rs. 300,000 per week for the first week, and includes testing of two ads, each with half of the total budget. The second week is typically a lower spend. Here we take time to thoroughly analyse the results from week one to identify the variables we'll test next. In weeks three and four, we continue testing with a budget in the Rs. 1,500,000 to Rs. 2,500,000 range. In total, you should plan to spend at Rs.1,000,000 to conduct initial testing that will provide you with guidance on the fundamental aspects of success in direct response radio: what works, with whom, and where.

This testing period isn't all just cost. The media spend during the testing period will generate calls and revenues.

The second phase for the media budget is the roll out, when you exceed your break even return on advertising. When you're operating at greater than break even profitability, you'll want your budget to grow because the more you spend on media, the greater your profit. That's the velocity effect of direct response radio advertising. Of course, there are logistical issues (inventory, manufacturing, fulfilment, etc.) that need to be ready for the increased volume. In the roll out phase, grow your budget at a rate that takes into account:

(a) Your business' readiness for growth.

(b) The building of a customised pool of profitable media for your campaign.

Number of Stations and Radio Ad Frequency

Now that you have a basic understanding of how to think about radio advertising costs, let's address the other two common sub-questions we get about radio advertising costs. "With my budget, how many radio stations will my ad run?" and "How many times will my spot air for that budget?"

The answer to both of these questions is the same: It depends. Generally, between six and ten radio stations will air the ads in the initial test budget. But, specifics get determined based on:

(a) Client preferences for speed of learning and client business volume constraints.

(b) The testing design and media plan—which are both determined in reviewing the product, target customers, and other information provided to us in a creative brief document.

Stations with larger audiences will cost more than stations with smaller audiences. We will test the number of stations we feel is necessary to answer the questions that yield the most information about what will work and what won't for your campaign. As far as the number of airings, direct response radio advertising has a range of optimum number of airings needed to deliver the highest return on advertising dollar. The key is to start within that optimum range, and then customise it to each campaign, format, and station using testing methodology. We've tested a large number of variables to determine the optimum schedule range—in terms of spot frequency as well as the distribution of spots across days of the week and dayparts. A good agency will have conducted similar data-driven research, and that's part of what you're buying when you hire an agency — their ability to arrive at the optimum schedule for you.

7

ONLINE ADVERTISING

Online advertising is all about advertising over the World Wide Web. In practice online advertising is about setting up an adwords account with Google and getting keyword based traffic to your website. Yes times are tough in the economy but people are using the Internet more and more with respect to shopping and if they find your products or services via keyword based research it is very likely that they will buy your offering.

BENEFITS OF ONLINE ADVERTISING

One major benefit of online advertising is the immediate publishing of information and content that is not limited by geography or time. To that end, the emerging area of interactive advertising presents fresh challenges for advertisers who have hitherto adopted an interruptive strategy. Another benefit is the efficiency of advertisers' investment. It means two facts, one is the customisation of advertisements, including content and posted websites. For example, AdWords, AdSense and Connecturf enable ads shown on relevant webpages or aside of search results of pre-chosen keywords. Another is the payment method. Whatever purchasing variation is selected, the payment is usually relative with audiences' response.

PURCHASING VARIATIONS

The three most common ways in which online advertising is purchased are CPM, CPV, CPC, and CPA.

- CPM (Cost Per Impression) is where advertisers pay for exposure of their message to a specific audience. CPM costs are priced per thousand impressions. The M in the acronym is the Roman numeral for one thousand.
- CPV (Cost Per Visitor) or (Cost per View in the case of Pop Ups and Unders) is where advertisers pay for the delivery of a Targeted Visitor to the advertisers website.
- CPC (Cost Per Click) is also known as Pay per click (PPC). Advertisers pay each time a user clicks on their listing and is redirected to their website. They do not actually pay for the listing, but only when the listing is clicked on. This system allows advertising specialists to refine searches and gain information about their market. Under the Pay per click pricing system, advertisers pay for the right to be listed under a series of target rich words that direct relevant traffic to their website, and pay only when someone clicks on their listing which links directly to their website. CPC differs from CPV in that each click is paid for regardless of whether the user makes it to the target site.
- CPA (Cost Per Action) or (Cost Per Acquisition) advertising is performance based and is common in the affiliate marketing sector of the business. In this payment scheme, the publisher takes all the risk of running the ad, and the advertiser pays only for the amount of users who complete a transaction, such as a purchase or sign-up. This is the best type of rate to pay for banner advertisements and the

worst type of rate to charge. Similarly, CPL (Cost Per Lead) advertising is identical to CPA advertising and is based on the user completing a form, registering for a newsletter or some other action that the merchant feels will lead to a sale. Also common, CPO (Cost Per Order) advertising is based on each time an order is transacted.

— Cost per conversion Describes the cost of acquiring a customer, typically calculated by dividing the total cost of an ad campaign by the number of conversions. The definition of "Conversion" varies depending on the situation: it is sometimes considered to be a lead, a sale, or a purchase.

— CPE (Cost Per Engagement) is a form of Cost Per Action pricing first introduced in March 2008. Differing from cost-per-impression or cost-per-click models, a CPE model means advertising impressions are free and advertisers pay only when a user engages with their specific ad unit. Engagement is defined as a user interacting with an ad in any number of ways.

Though, as seen above, the large majority of online advertising has a cost that is brought about by usage or interaction of an ad, there are a few other methods of advertising online that only require a one time payment. The Million Dollar Homepage is a very successful example of this. Visitors were able to pay Rs. 50 per pixel of advertising space and their advert would remain on the homepage for as long as the website exists with no extra costs.

— *Floating ad:* An ad which moves across the user's screen or floats above the content.

— *Expanding ad:* An ad which changes size and which may alter the contents of the webpage.

— *Polite ad:* A method by which a large ad will be downloaded in smaller pieces to minimise the disruption of the content being viewed.
— *Wallpaper ad:* An ad which changes the background of the page being viewed.
— *Trick banner:* A banner ad that looks like a dialog box with buttons. It simulates an error message or an alert.
— *Pop-up:* A new window which opens in front of the current one, displaying an advertisement, or entire webpage.
— *Pop-under:* Similar to a Pop-Up except that the window is loaded or sent behind the current window so that the user does not see it until they close one or more active windows.
— *Video ad:* similar to a banner ad, except that instead of a static or animated image, actual moving video clips are displayed.
— *Map ad:* text or graphics linked from, and appearing in or over, a location on an electronic map such as on Google Maps.
— *Mobile ad:* an SMS text or multi-media message sent to a cell phone.

In addition, ads containing streaming video or streaming audio are becoming very popular with advertisers.

Email Advertising

Legitimate Email advertising or E-mail marketing is often known as "opt-in e-mail advertising" to distinguish it from spam.

Affiliate Marketing

Affiliate marketing is a form of online advertising where advertisers place campaigns with a potentially large number of small (and large) publishers, whom are only paid media fees when traffic to the advertiser is garnered, and usually upon a specific measurable campaign result (a form, a sale, a sign-up, etc). Today, this is usually accomplished through contracting with an affiliate network or CPA network, such as Orkut, TradeDoubler, Neverblue, Performics, Hydra Network, Motive Interactive, Commission Junction/BeFree, LinkShare, Primeq, Consorte Media or Azoogle.

Affiliate marketing was an invention by CDNow.com in 1994 and was excelled by Amazon.com when it launched its Affiliate Programme, called Associate Programme in 1996. The online retailer used its programme to generate low cost brand exposure and provided at the same time small websites a way to earn some supplemental income.

Contextual Advertising

Many advertising networks display graphical or text-only ads that correspond to the keywords of an Internet search or to the content of the page on which the ad is shown. These ads are believed to have a greater chance of attracting a user, because they tend to share a similar context as the user's search query. For example, a search query for "flowers" might return an advertisement for a florist's website.

Another newer technique is embedding keyword hyperlinks in an article which are sponsored by an advertiser. When a user follows the link, they are sent to a sponsor's website.

Behavioural Targeting

In addition to contextual targeting, online advertising can be targeted based on a user's past clickstream. For example, if a user is known to have recently visited a number of automotive shopping/comparison sites based on clickstream analysis enabled by cookies stored on the user's computer, that user can then be served auto-related ads when they visit other, non-automotive sites.

Ads and Malware

There is also class of advertising methods which may be considered unethical and perhaps even illegal. These include external applications which alter system settings, spawn pop-ups, and insert advertisements into non-affiliated webpages. Such applications are usually labelled as spyware or adware. They may mask their questionable activities by performing a simple service, such as displaying the weather or providing a search bar. Some programmes are effectively trojans. These applications are commonly designed so as to be difficult to remove or uninstall. The ever-increasing audience of online users, many of whom are not computer-savvy, frequently lack the knowledge and technical ability to protect themselves from these programmes.

ETHICAL ISSUES IN ONLINE ADVERTISING

The web faces the same ethical issues as other media, plus a few of its own. Here are some rules for online ads.

When it comes to advertising, it's a given that making untrue claims, bait-and-switch offers, and the like are unethical. But those aren't the only ethical issues to consider. Advertorials, interstitial ads, pop-ups and pop-unders, contextual links, and overlay ads, to name a few, while not all unethical in and of themselves, all come with ethical hazards.

Why should an advertiser care about this? Because ethically questionable ads can have a negative impact on their brands. When users dislike an ad, they tend to extend that dislike to the advertiser. As web usability expert Jakob Nielsen puts it in an article on his web site: "Unethical ads will get you more fixations, but ethical business practices will attract more loyal customers in the long run."

Negative reactions can come from media companies too. They may be unwilling to accept certain ads because they will drive traffic away. The journalists' organisation The Poynter Institute, for instance, says in its online ethics guidelines: "The consumer's experience is paramount. Advertising models and sponsorships should be evaluated closely to determine their impact on consumer experience."

USING YOUR WEB SITE TO ADVERTISE YOUR BUSINESS

You can't hide from it. Whether you're driving by a billboard, listening to the radio or flipping through the TV channels, every advertisement has dot.com this and dot.com that.

Even in a lean economy, the evolution of the Internet has business taking a new direction. Now companies need a Web site even if they aren't involved in e-commerce. But this new wave of marketing still takes some old-school advertising.

Web sites need more than good content. A comprehensive advertising campaign is the only way to make a Web site successful. You not only have to tempt potential customers to buy from you but you have to tempt them to buy from you now!

There are several key factors you must consider to accomplish this:

What benefits does the customer get from buying the product? Does your product or service make people smarter, faster, more attractive?

State the benefits. And again.

It's the benefits that will hook your customer. And that hook will have them grabbing their credit card. But if they don't know what's in it for them, they'll be on your competitor's Web site faster than you can clear your cache files.

Keep your site updated. And give them a reason to come back.

Maybe weekly specials, new articles or post a newsletter. Make your site an invaluable resource. Giving people incentives to come back to your site can still generate sales even if the customer wasn't in the buying mood.

Do you have testimonials from your customers? Testimonials prove your product's worth as well as establish your company's credibility.

If you don't have testimonials, one way to get them is by donating your product or service to a few qualified customers. Let them know that you're giving them the product to try for a certain amount of time in exchange for their comments at the end of the trial period.

Make your Web page as easy to read as possible. Grab customers with powerful headlines.

The headlines gently ease customers to read further into your sales message without the tact of a used car salesman trying to unload a few lemons.

Headlines also break up the flow of copy, making your Web page easy on the eyes—something your customers will appreciate.

How many Web sites have you visited with grammatical errors or words misspelled? It looks unprofessional and makes would-be customers wonder about the professionalism of your company.

Proofread your Web page copy. Then have a few more people proofread it.

The writing needs to jump off the page. Fresh. Crisp. A poorly written Web page is worse than not having a Web page at all.

HOW TO CREATE A PODCAST AD

Podcasters are open to generating revenue but don't want to lose the quality of their podcast. Advertisers know podcasts are hot and it's not just small businesses that want to feature their ads in podcasts. Create a podcast ad that's designed to capture the listener's attention instead of being tuned out.

Selling Advertising for Your Podcast

Blogs have swept the Internet in popularity but it took a while for advertisers to take notice. However, podcasting has gained instant attention with the ad world and the reach they have is attracting everyone from small business advertisers to companies around the globe.

Research company eMarketer projects advertisers spent Rs. 4,000 million on podcasting advertising in 2006. By 2010, that number is expected to reach Rs.15,000 million.

Selling the space : Selling advertising in your podcast is much like selling advertising space on your Web site. Unlike selling a banner on a per-click basis, though, the most simple podcast ad can be inserted into your podcast and left there.

New companies on the horizon are giving the average podcaster an option to earn money. Fruitcast, Podbridge and Podtrac are ad-insertion companies helping podcasters gain revenue through podcasting ads.

Fruitcast and Podbridge split the revenue with the podcaster 50/50. Podtrac, on the other hand, keeps 25-percent of any revenue generated from podcasting ads.

New technology is being explored that allows performance-based audio ads to be used in podcasts. Most smaller podcasts won't have an immediate use for this technology just yet, though, if they're looking to control the types of ads that are put into their podcasts.

In the meantime, selling your podcasting ad space can be quite appealing since podcasts are generally free. This revenue can help you cover the cost of producing your podcast and create better content so you can gain even more listeners.

Commercial placement

Keep commercials limited and control their placement carefully. Some podcasters insert a commercial at the beginning of the podcast, some have a commercial in the middle and some have one at the end. Some even use the beginning, middle and end spaces to insert commercials.

Be sure you're not bombarding the listener with commercial after commercial, though. If you're producing a relatively short podcast of a few minutes, for example, a listener isn't going to want to hear three commercials in a small time frame. However, many podcasting experts warn against putting an ad at the beginning of your podcast. They say a commercial right off the top detracts from the listener's excitement of hearing your podcast. Instead of listening to your podcast right away, they have to hear a commercial first.

Commercial length

Most podcast listeners say they don't mind a 15-second commercial in their podcast. You definitely don't want to go off into a two-minute commercial break as if you're producing a radio broadcast. By keeping the commercial length short and limiting the placement, you can continue to serve your listeners first. You don't want to turn your podcast into a smattering of commercials that detracts from the hard work you put into your podcast and doesn't give your listeners anything valuable.

Who's listening?

Auto advertisers are really jumping on the podcast advertising bandwagon. Honda, Toyota, Lexus, Volvo and more are testing the podcasting waters.

A majority of podcasts aren't going to be able to gain these kinds of advertisers. What you can do instead is target those who may listen to your podcast.

By evaluating the type of podcast you're releasing, you're able to know who your potential advertisers are at the same time. You'll also want to know how many listeners your podcast has. Advertisers will want to know how many people their ad could potentially reach before buying the space.

Podcasting ad rates

The value of a podcast is hard for both podcasters and advertisers to gage this early in the game. Audible's WordCast is providing a service that allows podcasters to see how many people are downloading your podcast to help you establish an advertising rate card.

The service charges the podcaster up to five and a half cents per podcast download. The info WordCast gathers helps the podcaster determine exactly who the listeners are and what's they're downloading.

Sponsorships over advertising

An alternative to podcast advertising is to find a sponsor

for your podcast. Georgia-Pacific entered into a six-figure deal with a parenting podcast called Mommycast. A 15-year-old girl in Texas has sponsors for her EmoGirlTalk podcast that include an acne treatment product called Nature's Cure and the domain name provider GoDaddy.com.

Sponsorships generally have the podcaster mentioning the sponsor within the podcast. Don't underestimate the value of a sponsor. Many podcasters have found more success by getting a solid sponsor than selling podcast advertising space on a regular basis.

No matter how you pursue advertising for your podcast, just make sure your content doesn't suffer. Otherwise, you won't gain any new listeners and you'll lose the following you had, ultimately losing your advertisers in the process.

CPA-BASED WEB ADVERTISING

In the jargon-filled world of online advertising, CPA—cost-per-action—advertising may seem confusing at first. Also known as "pay for performance," CPA is an effective way for advertisers to select how they want to pay for their advertising—by click, impression, sale, or other variable.

Pay-for-click advertising is very popular, but it can be costly. As such, it may be out of reach for many businesses. If you prefer to pay by sale, CPA-based advertising can deliver your customers to you and guarantee that you won't pay a dime unless until you make a sale. In the highly competitive and expensive world of Internet advertising, this is a rare bit of insurance for your company?s advertising budget.

But sales aren't the only "actions" you can choose to pay for. If you offer registrations or subscriptions on your site, a CPA-based programme can be very effective. If you are simply seeking new leads for your company by using an opt-in mailing list, you can utilise CPA-based advertising to guarantee interested leads.

The benefit of CPA advertising is obvious—you get what you pay for. And your ads will generally run in more places for longer if you decide to pay only for specified actions. This can translate to greater visibility for your company.

Now that you know what CPA-based advertising is, how does it work? When you place your ad with a CPA agency, or through a site that offers the ability to run CPA ads, your ad will begin to display as soon as it is added to the rotation.

First, you will need to decide what actions you are willing to pay for. You can use the traditional pay-per-click option, or pay by sale or by registration, whichever fits your advertising budget.

Once your ad begins to display, it will be in the rotation until the set amount of actions have transpired. If you require 100 sales from an ad campaign, your ad will display until you have reached 100 sales.

Here are a few instances where a CPA campaign might make sense.

- *Testing your ads before starting a large campaign:* CPA lets you see just how many customers actually purchase your products after viewing your ad. Even if you decide to take your campaign to a CPC- or CPM-based outlet later, you can fine-tune it ahead of time by using CPA-based advertising.
- *Testing an affiliate programme:* Since affiliate programmes are essentially CPA-based advertising campaigns, you can test the waters ahead of time,

without having to worry about long term affiliate arrangements.

— *Poor ad performance:* If you have been experiencing slow sales or a lack of response from your current advertising programmes, it may be time to give CPA-based advertising a try.

— *Limited advertising budget:* CPA-based advertising is also an effective way of reaching new customers without having to expend unnecessary advertising resources. You will be able to set not only the action that you will pay for, but also the amount you are willing to pay for this action.

As with any ad campaign, there is no silver bullet, and no one way approach can be right for everyone. Try a number of different approaches, and keep careful track of the results. Only then will you know which ads will deliver the best return on your advertising investment.

In a CPM campaign, you pay for each how many times the ad appears. If your ad performs well and lots of users click through to your site, then each click-through costs you less. On the other hand, the lower the click-through rate, the more each click costs you.

CPC advertising protects you by fixing the amount you pay for each click, and sets a ceiling on how much you'll pay. By paying only for actual clicks, you save money and reach only targeted customers. Gone are the days of paying for thousands of impressions that are uselessly displayed. This is a great way for businesses to control their advertising budget and gauge response to their advertising campaigns.

For example, if you decide to advertise with a CPC-based search engine or a featured listing with a search engine, your ad will display each time a user enters in a keyword that matches your predetermined keyword list.

You don't pay each time the ad displays; only when it's actually clicked.

If you prefer to try CPC-based banner advertising, the principle is the same. Your ad will display and each time it is clicked on by an end user, you get charged. Your ad runs until you have reached a predetermined amount of actual clicks. This means that your ad may get much more exposure than it would using a traditional impressions calculation method.

These extra impressions allow your ad to stay up longer, which may mean that even if you do not receive click-throughs right away, you may end up with users who decide to visit your site later on.

CPC-based advertising allows businesses to pay only for the targeted leads they receive. In the competitive online marketplace, this can spell success much more quickly than other advertising methods.

Whether your company has successfully used CPC-based methods in the past, or if you are completely new to the idea, there are several places where you can find CPC-based advertising.

Google AdWords is one of the most well known CPC-based advertising venues. With AdWords, you pick the keywords you want to use and only pay for as many clicks as you can afford. Instead of having to pay for a campaign that may be more costly than you had planned, you can set a limit on the amount of times your ad can be clicked and cap the total amount you'll spend on the campaign. This can be a life saver for a company that cannot risk an advertising campaign that may result in thousands of dollars of unexpected advertising bills.

If you prefer banner advertising, there are also myriad companies offering CPC-based banner ads in addition to the traditional CPM advertising method.

CPC advertising is clearly here to stay. But don't spend all your ad dollars in one place. Test different methods of advertising at the same time, and always track the results. This is the only way to determine what works for you, and the only way to get the most for your advertising spend.

INTERNET ADVERTISING MISTAKES

Ten of the most common mistakes with some tips on how to avoid them.

1. *Wasting money:* No business owner wants to throw their money away on ineffective ads, but many still do. Business owners routinely spend money to advertise on Web sites that generate lots of unique hits but do not draw paying customers to their businesses. Track the effectiveness of your advertising campaigns, and discontinue advertising on any site that does not deliver quality leads that convert into sales.
2. *Paying for pop-ups:* Pop-up ads generally are not effective. In fact, they may turn away rather than attract your prospects. The growing popularity and effectiveness of pop-up blocking utilities make buying pop-ups a losing proposition.
3. *Spamming:* If you are sending unwanted emails, you may be sending SPAM, which can ultimately hurt your business. Email marketing is possibly the most effective tool in your arsenal, but it must be used properly. You should generally market only to people who have opted in to your mailings.
4. *Overspending on copywriters:* Web copywriting is not rocket science. A smart, creative young copywriter with fresh ideas can often do a comparable or better job than a veteran writer. There is no

shortage of young writers looking to build a portfolio of their work If you are working with a copywriter and not getting the results you want, try another writer.

2. *Favoring style over substance:* Most advertising puts style ahead of substance, but Internet advertising is an extreme case. Flash animation and other high-tech ?glitter? is no substitute for saying something significant about your product or service.

6. *No call to action:* For an ad to be effective, you must tell people what to do. Putting your name in front of your target audience on a regular basis is half the battle, the next step is letting them know what you want them to do. A call to action can be as simple "Click here to learn more," but every ad should have one.

7. *Stale advertising:* The same boring ad does not enhance your brand, and it may even damage your brand equity. While an established brand, slogan or logo could be your trademark for many years, you still need to remain current and continue to include creative variations on a theme.

8. *Not utilising all your online opportunities:* While you never want to "junk up" your site or your newsletter with too many ads, you need to strategically place advertisements and promotion in the right places for the best results. Too often, page headers and footers and other key locations are underutilised. Advertising your own products, both on- and offline, is critical.

9. *Not being viewer-friendly:* Just as your Web site should be user friendly, it should also be easy on the eyes. Readers should be able to get the intended message clearly without being distracted

by flashing ads, imposing blocks of text, or other design faux-pas.

10. *Poor placement:* If you do not know where your ad will be placed, do not spend a dime on it. When you purchase advertising on a Web site or in a newsletter, find out exactly where and when your ads will appear. Make sure your ad appears as it should, appears where you wanted it to, and when you expected it to run. Follow-up and tracking are critical to any advertising campaign.

8

SMALL BUSINESS ADVERTISING

Advertising plays an important role in successful business ventures. It entails identifying and selecting the media that provide the greatest amount of exposure for your business and developing effective, yet appropriate materials for each medium. It is more than running an ad in a local newspaper, on a radio or television station or just simply hanging a sign outside your business and waiting for the customers to purchase your product. It requires that you know your product—that is, the selling points—and that you develop literature that can arouse the customers' consciousness levels to the point that they are curious enough to investigate it, and then raises their need or desire levels to the point that they are willing to purchase it.

Advertising keeps your product or service in the public's eye by creating a sense of awareness. Yet this awareness alone will not ensure the success of your business. Thus, advertising not only has to be effective, it also has to be a continuous process.

It may be a good idea to mix the different media formats that you use. For example, design a brochure that describes your product, emphasizing its selling points (special features). Place copies of the brochure in strategic locations of your business to use as customer handouts. Or, devise a customer survey. The survey should focus on whether customers like the product, the quality of the product, ways to improve it, the quality of service provided by staff—their friendliness and courtesy. Place the survey with a self-addressed, stamped envelope near the check-out counter and ask customers to mail in or return the survey when they come back. Review their comments with staff and implement those suggestions that are practical, cost efficient and can improve the overall quality of service your business provides.

MEDIA FORMATS

Newspaper, radio, or television ads (newspaper advertising is the least expensive and television advertising is the most expensive of these formats). You probably will need professional advice and assistance when developing ads for those media formats. The following media formats you probaly can do yourself:

- Business cards.
- Classified ads in the local newspapers.
- Direct marketing.
- Telemarketing (this format can be expensive, also).
- Yellow Pages advertising.
- Sampling—mailing or distributing free samples of your product to the public.
- Advertising in community-based magazines or newspapers.

Whatever media format you use, be willing to invest the money needed to develop an effective ad campaign.

PROMOTIONS

Promotion entails more than just selecting the media format to market your business. It can, and oftentimes does, encompass community involvement. This involvement can range from sponsoring a Boy or Girl Scout or NCC troop to hosting a charity ball for senior citizens or allowing non-profit organisations to use your facilities.

Your approach to promoting your business should encompass more than creating a sense of awareness about your business. It should include a commitment to community involvement—the desire to give something back to the community and its residents. An excellent way to foster this type of involvement is to meet with community leaders to find out how you can help, and what events are forthcoming that could or will require your assistance. Keep in mind that community leaders can be an excellent networking tool, especially if they feel your involvement is genuine.

Examples of community programmes you can sponsor or take part in are:

— Sponsor a Boy or Girl Scout or NCC troop for summer camp.

— Sponsor a underprivileged child in day camp.

— Host and sponsor a charity ball for senior citizens.

— Sponsor cooperative education for high school and/or college students.

— Volunteer as a tutor for at-risk (those likely to drop out or fail in school) students.

— Sponsor a fund raiser for the homeless, or day care tuition assistance for children of single-parent households.

— Offer summer employment to local high school, middle school and college students.

— Volunteer in a local literacy programme.

Other inexpensive ways of promoting your business that doesn't encompass community involvement are:

— Employee tee shirts, hats, aprons or jackets with the name of your business and logo.

— Ball point pens with the name, telephone number and logo of your business.

— Balloons with the name, telephone number and logo of your business.

— Free samples.

— A door prize for the 100th or 1,000th customer to enter your business.

While it is impossible for you to participate in every event or programme in the community, you should at least get involved in one or two activities, even if it's only on a part-time basis. People tend to be more supportive of businesses, organisations or individuals who give something to the community. And, this is the image you especially want to project in your promotional activities.

No plan that anyone provides will show you how to promote or advertise your business. These are techniques that you, yourself, will have to develop. Talk it over with your family and community leaders, then decide which activities you can afford to sponsor and have the time to commit to before becoming involved. Involvement in the community doesn't necessarily have a price tag attached. Find a project that you can afford, that you have time for and is of interest to you.

LAWS OF SMALL BUSINESS ADVERTISING SUCCESS

Small business advertising is a science and an art. Companies often miss the fundamentals of advertising. Regardless of the size of your business an understanding of the laws of advertising can reap huge rewards. A 5% small business advertising budget can only help if you understand the laws of advertising. The following are the six laws of small business advertising success:

1. *Use one message:* A high response rate ad usually conveys a single message. Your small business advertising needs to quickly communicate its core message in three seconds or less.
2. *Add credibility:* It has become human nature to distrust advertising. Claims need to be real and credible.
3. *Test everything:* Large businesses have a greater margin to waste capital and resources without testing advertising. Small businesses do not have the luxury. Use coupons, codes, and specials to measure the headline, timing, and placement of your ad. Test only one item at a time and one medium. Testing can be as simple as asking every customer for several weeks how they heard of your business.
4. *Be easy to contact:* Every single brochure, box, email and all company literature should have full contact information including: website and email address, phone and fax numbers, and company address. It seems simple but is forgotten by most companies.
5. *Match ads to target:* Successful business advertising speaks to one target market only. An ad in a medical publication preached the cardio-vascular benefits of cross-country skiing to heart patients.

Ads in women's magazines discussed the weight-loss and calorie burn from cross-country skiing. Focus the message to the target group.

6. *Create curiosity:* Successful business advertising does not sell a product or service. Fo instance, NordicTrack's ads sold the free video. Once a potential customer watched the video, they contacted the company for more information. The end result, millions of dollars of sales. Create ads that generate interest and make the customer want more information.

Having a poor response is not the medium's fault. Often the problem is the message. Small business advertising is not a quick fix solution to marketing your company. It takes planning, testing and constant exposure to have an impact on your small business. Done correctly, small business advertising can be a winning strategy.

ADVERTISING IDEAS FOR SMALL BUSINESSES

Small Business Advertising Beyond Word-of- Mouth

Word of mouth is excellent small business advertising – but it's slow, and may be practically non-existent for new businesses. If you want to grow your customer base more quickly, you have to advertise. This collection of small business advertising ideas presents both the tried and true and advertising ideas you may not have tried yet – advertising ideas for your small business to effectively reach your target market and attract new customers.

Tried and true small business advertising ideas

1. *The yellow pages:* There's still a lot of people who use the yellow pages to find the businesses they're looking for – and they won't find you if your small

business isn't listed there. Get the biggest yellow page ad you can afford; the more visibility the better.

2. *Newspaper advertising:* Besides box ads and advertising inserts, local newspapers also often offer special advertising features showcasing particular businesses – all powerful small business advertising opportunities. Don't overlook special interest newspapers as an advertising idea if they exist in your area. They may be delivered to exactly the audience you want to reach.
3. *Direct mail:* Direct mail can be very effective small business advertising—and is much more favourably received than other direct marketing media, such as email or telemarketing. And even if you don't have a mailing list, you can still geographically target your mail.
4. *Magazine advertising:* This advertising idea can be a very effective way of reaching a target market. The trick is to choose the magazines or e-zines that best match the market you're targeting.
5. *Business cards:* Sure, they're advertising. Every time you hand one out to a prospective client or customer, you're advertising your small business. But why not take this advertising idea further and Make Your Business Card a Marketing Vehicle?
6. *Joining professional/business organisations:* Every professional or business organisation offers exclusive advertising opportunities for their members, ranging from free promotion on the organisation's website through special section newspaper advertising. And being a member can be good small business advertising in itself.

7. *Vehicle advertising:* The reason you see so many vehicles emblazoned with advertising is that it works; vehicle advertising is very visible small business advertising. If you're not ready for custom graphics or a magnet quad sign that sit atop your vehicle, go for a magnetic sign that you can take off when you want.

Advertising ideas you may not have tried yet

8. *Sending promos with invoices:* Little advertising ideas can be powerful, too. If you're sending out an invoice, why not take the opportunity to include some small business advertising? To draw new customers, try something such as a "bring-a-friend" promotion.
9. *Cable TV advertising:* So you can't afford to advertise your business during the Super Bowl. That doesn't mean you have to miss out on the household reach of TV. Cable TV companies offer advertising ideas within the budget of small businesses, from advertising on the TV Guide Listings or Real Estate channels through running infomercials.
10. *Radio advertising:* Another advertising idea you may not have thought of is radio advertising. Running ads on a local radio station can be both effective and relatively inexpensive.
11. *Bench/bus stop advertising:* Looking to reach a mass audience? Then transit advertising may be the best advertising idea for you. Contact your local transit company for information on bench, bus and shelter advertising possibilities.
12. *Local website advertising:* More people are spending more time online than ever before. Cover all your small business advertising bases by ensuring that your business is listed on websites providing

business information for your local area. Many municipalities, for instance, offer business listings on their sites.

13. *Trade show participation:* One of the main reasons to participate in trade shows is to be seen and get known. While participating in big trade shows can be quite expensive, there are a lot of smaller opportunities that may work well for your business, from trade shows put on by local business associations through trade shows focused on particular industries.
14. *Email advertising:* If you already have an in-house mailing list or are able to develop one, email advertising can work for you.
15. *Community involvement:* Visible, tangible involvement with your community is more than good PR; it's also very effective small business advertising. So choose a charitable event or community association to get involved with and let yourself be seen as a business that cares.
16. *Cross-promotion:* Joining forces with other businesses can greatly increase your advertising power and your marketing reach. Kare Anderson explains how this advertising idea works and how to jump-start your cross-promotion efforts in Attract More Customers through Cross-Promotion.
17. *eBay listings:* eBay can be a fast and inexpensive way to make your potential customers aware of your products. When you list an item for auction, you're also advertising your business to whoever views the listing.

Will all of these seventeen advertising ideas work for your small business? No! But by choosing several of these advertising ideas and focusing on them, you'll be able to grow your customer base much more quickly than you would by relying on word-of-mouth alone. Like any kind of marketing you do, of course, your small business advertising will be most effective if you plan your advertising campaign and track your results.

9

COVERT ADVERTISING

Covert advertising includes a range of different marketing tactics that don't announce themselves as advertising. Product placement in films, celebrity endorsement of big name brands, sponsorship of sporting events etc. are all examples of covert advertising. Many companies now pay film producers to have their products featured in films. Believe it or not, covert advertising is an established part of the financing of Hollywood films. There are even certain companies whose sole responsibility is to guarantee product placement in films for particular brands.

Businesses need covert advertising because it is a tactic that simply works. It puts money in the pockets of businesses. A company can definitely increase its profits using this type of advertising. Just think about some of your favorite movies and what products were placed in them without you consciously being aware of them. Many companies also use covert advertising on commercial radio.

IMPLEMENTING COVERT ADVERTISING

If you have a business that can afford covert advertising on television, radio, or the movies, then you have people who will make sure that your business will properly implement covert advertising. If you are a small business owner, don't fret. Believe it or not, there are still many ways you can implement covert advertising into your business plan. Write an article for a local newspaper. In this format, you need to sneak in your product or specialty as part of the solution to your article. Be sure to include a link at the bottom of the article that gives your name, phone number, and website.

Don't have too much pride to ask a colleague to plug you and your product. If you make cookies, have a friend take the cookies to work and place them at their desk. When people ask about the cookies or better yet, try one, have your friend give them your contact information.

In these days, you can have acquaintances use covert advertising in their blogs for you. Covert advertising has proved to stand the test of time. It is a tactic that has netted large profits for many businesses. So whether you're a small business or a large business, it's definitely to your financial benefit to give covert advertising a try.

COVERT ADVERTISING AND MARKETING

Covert advertising techniques are the opposite of overt advertising techniques. Overt advertising is the typical blatant advertising found in magazines and newspapers, on television, on billboards, on leaflets, and in film trailers. Covert advertising is sneakier and it is cheaper.

Typical Covert Advertising Techniques

Product placement within films and on television programmes

If a film or television programme contains many visual references to a certain product then you can be pretty certain that product is buying covert advertising on the show or in the film. e.g. Nokia phones were used extensively in Charlie's Angels and The *Matrix*; the Bond movies use product placement extensively e.g. cars, alcohol, watches, phones, aftershave; in TV soaps particular brands of food products and perfumes are often shown.

Advantages of product placement are:

- You have a captive audience.
- It is cheaper than overt advertising or sponsorship.
- If the programme or film is a success your advertising gets a wider audience.
- The product becomes linked to the film or programme and the ideology/lifestyle inherent in that text. This attracts people to buy into the image through the product.
- It is difficult to filter out.
- Has an immediate effect but it can be short term.

Sponsorship of television programmes

In some countries this was only recently introduced in 1995. Now we see 'The Premiership'sponsored by Coca-cola, 'Coronation Street' sponsored by Cadbury and 'Blind Date' sponsored by Muller (yoghurt) to name a few. American programmes have been sponsored for many years and now we also see 'Friends' sponsored by Jacob's Creek (wine) and 'The Simpsons' sponsored by Dominoes Pizza (the sponsorship is different in the USA). Sponsorship is a covert technique because it is not actually advertising overtly, the sponsorship advert is usually entertaining, it is never a hard sell and it is never very informative. Sponsorship hopes to link the product more directly to the film or programme and it is more expensive than product placement but also more effective.

The advantages of sponsorship are similar to product placement.

Plugging products

Plugs occur in many places.

- In supermarkets reps plug products by getting you to try them before you buy them.
- In cinemas, restaurants and pubs you may get special promotional offers to encourage you to buy a product.
- One of the more controversial plugging attempts was the regular plugging of Marlboro cigarettes, which were given away in student pubs, in some western countries.
- Celebrities can also be used to plug products e.g., Sharukh Khan wearing Belmont clothes.

Promotional plugging

On television chat shows people plug their new film, book, record or product. This is basically free advertising. This is different to a covert plug technique by a corporate company.

The advantages of plugging are:

- Consumers feel happy because they have a cheap or free product.
- It's a quick way to get people using or thinking about your product.
- Plugging is 'hands on' advertising; people can't just ignore it like they can in magazines or on television.

Viral Marketing

The term viral marketing was originally penned in a

newsletter by venture capitalist Steve Jurvetson, who defined it as "network-enhanced word of mouth." While the word "viral" may have negative connotations, the concept of viral marketing is a positive one.

Marketers have long believed that people who hear about a product or service from a friend are more likely to buy, and buy more quickly and easily than those who heard about it in other ways. In fact, many women who told two friends, and then "they told two friends, and so on and so on and so on."

While that commercial is probably the easiest way to illustrate the concept of viral marketing, it's not the most helpful example because: (1) most of us can't afford to produce a TV commercial, and (2) now, with the Internet, and email in particular, you can tell more people about something faster than good-oldfashioned word of mouth.

Principles of Viral Marketing

The term "viral marketing" is offensive. Call yourself a Viral Marketer and people will take two steps back. I would. "Do they have a vaccine for that yet?" you wonder. A sinister thing, the simple virus is fraught with doom, not quite dead yet not fully alive, it exists in that nether genre somewhere between disaster movies and horror flicks.

But you have to admire the virus. He has a way of living in secrecy until he is so numerous that he wins by sheer weight of numbers. He piggybacks on other hosts and uses their resources to increase his tribe. And in the right environment, he grows exponentially. A virus don't even have to mate—he just replicates, again and again with geometrically increasing power, doubling with each iteration:

1

11

1111

11111111

1111111111111111

11111111111111111111111111111111

1111111111111111111111111111111111111111111111111111111111111111

In a few short generations, a virus population can explode.

The classic example of viral marketing is Hotmail.com, one of the first free Webbased e-mail services. The strategy is simple:

1. Give away free e-mail addresses and services,
2. Attach a simple tag at the bottom of every free message sent out: "Get your private, free email at http://www.hotmail.com",
3. Then stand back while people e-mail to their own network of friends and associates,
4. Who see the message,
5. Sign up for their own free e-mail service, and then
6. Propel the message still wider to their own ever-increasing circles of friends and associates.

Like tiny waves spreading ever farther from a single pebble dropped into a pond, a carefully designed viral marketing strategy ripples outward extremely rapidly.

Elements of a Viral Marketing Strategy

Accept this fact. Some viral marketing strategies work better than others, and few work as well as the simple Hotmail.com strategy. But below are the six basic elements you hope to include in your strategy. A viral marketing strategy need not contain ALL these elements, but the more elements it embraces, the more powerful the results are likely to be. An effective viral marketing strategy:

1. Gives away products or services.
2. Provides for effortless transfer to others.
3. Scales easily from small to very large.
4. Exploits common motivations and behaviours.
5. Utilises existing communication networks.
6. Takes advantage of others' resources.

Gives away Valuable Products or Services

"Free" is the most powerful word in a marketer's vocabulary. Most viral marketing programmes give away valuable products or services to attract attention. Free e-mail services, free information, free "cool" buttons, free software programmes that perform powerful functions but not as much as you get in the "pro" version. Wilson's Second Law of Web Marketing is "The Law of Giving and Selling". "Cheap" or "inexpensive" may generate a wave of interest, but "free" will usually do it much faster. Viral marketers practice delayed gratification. They may not profit today, or tomorrow, but if they can generate a groundswell of interest from something free, they know they will profit "soon and for the rest of their lives". Patience, my friends. Free attracts eyeballs. Eyeballs then see other desirable things that you are selling, and, presto! you earn money. Eyeballs bring valuable e-mail addresses, advertising revenue, and e-commerce sales opportunities. Give away something, sell something.

Provides for Effortless Transfer to Others

Public health nurses offer sage advice at flu season: stay

away from people who cough, wash your hands often, and don't touch your eyes, nose, or mouth. Viruses only spread when they're easy to transmit. The medium that carries your marketing message must be easy to transfer and replicate: e-mail, website, graphic, software download. Viral marketing works famously on the Internet because instant communication has become so easy and inexpensive. Digital format make copying simple. From a marketing standpoint, you must simplify your marketing message so it can be transmitted easily and without degradation. Short is better.

Scales Easily from Small to Very Large

To spread like wildfire the transmission method must be rapidly scalable from small to very large. The weakness of the Hotmail model is that a free e-mail service requires its own mailservers to transmit the message. If the strategy is wildly successful, mailservers must be added very quickly or the rapid growth will bog down and die. If the virus multiplies only to kill the host before spreading, nothing is accomplished. So long as you have planned ahead of time how you can add mailservers rapidly you're okay. You must build in scalability to your viral model.

Exploits Common Motivations and Behaviours

Clever viral marketing plans take advantage of common human motivations. What proliferated "Netscape Now" buttons in the early days of the Web? The desire to be cool. Greed drives people. So does the hunger to be popular, loved, and understood. The resulting urge to communicate produces millions of websites and billions of email messages. Design a marketing strategy that builds on common motivations and behaviours for its transmission, and you have a winner.

Utilises Existing Communication Networks

Most people are social. Nerdy, basement-dwelling computer science grad students are the exception. Social scientists tell us that each person has a network of 8 to 12 people in their close network of friends, family, and associates. A person's broader network may consist of scores, hundreds, or thousands of people, depending upon her position in society. A waitress, for example, may communicate regularly with hundreds of customers in a given week. Network marketers have long understood the power of these human networks, both the strong, close networks as well as the weaker networked relationships. People on the Internet develop networks of relationships, too. They collect e-mail addresses and favorite website URLs. Affiliate programmes exploit such networks, as do permission e-mail lists. Learn to place your message into existing communications between people, and you rapidly multiply its dispersion.

Takes Advantage of Others' Resources

The most creative viral marketing plans use others' resources to get the word out. Affiliate programmes, for example, place text or graphic links on others' websites. Authors who give away free articles, seek to position their articles on others' webpages. A news release can be picked up by hundreds of periodicals and form the basis of articles seen by hundreds of thousands of readers. Now someone else's newsprint or webpage is relaying your marketing message. Someone else's resources are depleted rather than your own.

Guerilla Marketing

Coined by Jay Conrad Levinson, Guerilla marketing is a business strategy which begins with the position that every contact between business and customer is a marketing opportunity. This means guerrilla marketing can target niche (rather than mass) audiences, using specialised (rather than mass) media. In other words, it is typically not a mass media technique and therefore not really a subject for media students. The mass media usually only gets involved when a guerrilla marketing tactic becomes a news story. The following notes are included for your interest, and to complete your picture of 21st Century marketing techniques.

Guerrilla marketing means marketing that is unconventional, non-traditional, refusing to accept traditional rules of engagement, and extremely flexible.

Key Guerilla marketing principles

1. Guerilla marketing is about time, energy, imagination and knowledge, rather than money.
2. Strategies are informed by psychology and known patterns of human behaviour rather than guesswork and opinion.
3. Profits are the only measure of success, and are grown by building relationships with customers..
4. Guerrilla marketing was created for small businesses.
5. Guerilla marketers are devoted to customer follow-up.
6. They deploy multiple strategies rather than single, narrow campaigns.
7. Guerrillas aim at individuals, not groups.
8. Guerrillas embrace technology.
9. All Guerrilla marketing is intentional, from how the phone is answered to the clothes that Guerrillas wear.

10

SCOPE OF ADVERTISING IN INDIA

Advertising has been defined as any paid form for non-personal presentation and promotion of ideas, goods or services by an identified sponsor and more narrowly as any human communication intended to persuade or influence buyers in their purchase decisions. It lies at the juncture where culture and the economy interact: its primary purpose is to sell products and services by stimulating purchasing behaviour and it does this by using strategies that rework culture, creating aspirations and new desires for products.

At its inception, advertising was merely an announcement; for example, entrepreneurs in ancient Egypt used criers to announce ship and cargo arrivals. The invention of printing, however, may be said to have ushered in modern advertising. After the influence of salesmanship began to insert itself into public notice in the 18th century, the present elaborate form of advertising began to evolve. The advertising agencies, working on a commission basis, has been chiefly responsible for this evolution. The largest group of advertisers are the food marketers, followed by marketers of drugs and cosmetics, soaps, automobiles, tobacco, appliances, and oil products.

The major criticisms of advertising are that it creates false values and impels people to buy things they neither need nor want and that, in fact, may be actually harmful (such as cigarettes). In reply, its defenders say that advertising is meant to sell products, not create values; that it can create a new market for products that fill a genuine, though latent, need; and that it furthers product improvement through free competition.

Advertising in India is a highly competitive business. Today with the increasing consumer awareness no business can survive for long without advertising with growing business competition it has become necessary to ensure right media mix to each target audience. Today, advertising agencies are precisely taking care of consumer needs and provide creative designs with concept and ideas.

Advertisers in India reach about 75 percent of the population through television, and almost the entire population through radio. Certain televised programmes enjoy a viewership of more than 100 million. The Indian viewership exhibits a brand name recognition of both foreign and domestic products and services.

With value added information such as television rating points, audience profiles, and opinion polls available to marketers, the sophistication of advertising in India is at par with world standards. The world's leading advertising agencies—Ogilvy & Mather, J W Thompson, BBDO, Young & Rubican, Lintas, McCann Ericsson, Leo Burnett and a host of others —all have a major presence in the Indian market. The major Indian advertising media are newspapers, magazines, television and radio, business publications and billboards.

In India, the scope for advertising has progressed considerably with big names dealing in various businesses coming forward to showcase their specialties through advertising. In fact, a lot of capital and expertise goes on to the industry to make it a viable pasture for grazing. There is stiff competition in the industry and the existence is very tough. An Indian advertising agency has to take a lot of factors into consideration taking care not to cross the line of discomfort for the consumers.

Advertising on the internet is the most cost-efficient way of reaching customers all over the world including India. Indian advertising agencies need to wake up to the challenges posed by global economic trends and emerging interactive technologies like the Internet, Indian companies need to pay attention to characteristics of the new economy like open standards, digitalisation, and volatility, as Internet-based communication offers "tremendous new opportunities for Indian companies via media convergence and re-intermediation. This also requires Indian advertising agencies to pay attention to the importance of online market research, since new media like the net are bound to affect people's perceptions of advertising. The challenge for Indian advertising agencies in the coming years is to be able to target the rural market as well as the sophisticated urban market who may have Internet access.

GROWTH OF INDIAN ADVERTISING INDUSTRY

There has been a long tradition of advertising in India since the first newspapers published in India in the 19th Century carried advertising. The first advertising agency was established in 1905, B. Datram and Company, followed by The India-Advertising Company in 1907, the Calcutta Advertising agency in 1909, S.H.Bensen in 1928, J. Walter Thompson Associates through its Indian associate, Hindustan Thompson Associates in 1929, Lintas (Lever International Advertising Services) in 1939 and McCann Erikson in 1956. Under the more socialist political environment of the 1960s and 1970s there was little incentive for companies to advertise because advertising was not tax deductible. In the 1970s there was a 58 per cent growth in the number of registered agencies from 106 in 1969 to 168 in 1979, and this included a growth in Indian agencies. The first advertising appeared on state television in 1976. With the opening of the economy in the 1980s there was a growth in the number of alliances with multinational agencies and an expansion in advertising though foreign network participation in agency ownership was limited. In 1987 Hindustan Thompson was affiliated to J. Walter Thompson. Lintas, the 2nd ranking agency, held only 4 per cent of its subsidiary, as did Ogilvy and Mather. Saatchi and Saatchi/Compton had minority interests in Compton as did Lintas. A study done in 1984 of the largest companies in India found that the ratio of advertising expenditure to sales had risen from .64 in 1976, to .71 in 1980 to .74 in 1984. Foreign controlled corporations had the dominant share of total advertising expenditure, and 80 per cent of these were in the consumer goods sectors.

Advertising was very concentrated with the top 50 advertisers accounting for 80 per cent of the advertising spending and the top 10 advertisers made up 40 per cent of that figure, 32 per cent of the total. The largest advertiser throughout the period was Hindustan Lever, Rs.28.9 million in 1976, Rs. 29.1 million in 1980 and Rs. 80.9 million in 1984 which was nearly 10 per cent of the advertising budget of the corporate sector companies. Pharmaceutical companies were also significant advertisers at this time. Advertising expenditure grew at nearly 15 per cent a year in the 1980s to reach Rs. 44,800 million by the end of the decade.

There was a massive expansion in advertising in India in the mid 1990s and increased competition among multinationals made big budgets a necessity. New entrants in the market, for example Samsung, had to spend heavily to raise brand awareness. Advertising expenditure in 1996 was Rs. 52600 million and in 2001

Rs. 87400 million. These increases are also reflected in per capita growth in 2005, 2006 and 2007, though expenditure is still very low compared to other countries.

ADVERTISING AGENCIES

The profile of advertising agencies in India changed dramatically in the 1990s. Prior to that advertising was dominated by Indian agencies, but foreign agencies have increasingly come to dominate Indian advertising. In 1992-1993 11 of the top 20 Indian agencies were affiliated with multinational agencies and those agencies were allowed to own stock in the local companies since the early 1990s. In 1990 the key companies that were the top advertisers in India were also the leading advertisers internationally: Hindustan Unilever, Procter and Gamble and Nestle. In 1992-3 the monopoly of a small range of product categories was associated with a few companies which dominated advertising. Hindustan Unilever had a major impact on the content of programming and the initiation of new programmes, associated with their power as the major advertiser on television

In 1996-1997 over half of the advertising expenditure came from multinational corporations. South Korean companies are among the prominent new entries into the Indian marketplace. Procter and Gamble and automobile companies are noticeably absent from the list of top companies. The largest spender on advertising in 1995/96 was International Tobacco Corporation, which is interesting given the restrictions on tobacco advertising on television. In 1996 the top product category was still personal care products. The companies with the largest advertising budgets in India were: International Tobacco Corporation (cigarette and tobacco products); Hindustan Unilever Ltd. (personal care); Videocon International (electronics); Brook Bond Lipton, (diversified products); Colgate Palmolive (personal care); Philips (electronics);

Indexport (personal care); Hindustan Times (newspapers); Godfrey Philips (cigarette and tobacco products); Nestle (food, dairy products).

The advertising industry has expanded again rapidly in recent years. Growth was 23 per cent in 2000-2001 and the top 5 agencies in 2000-2001 earned 47.2 per cent of total revenue. Foreign companies were seen to be initiating more aggressive advertising campaigns and recent growth in advertising has been driven by television advertising, especially satellite channels many of which are free-to-air which means they rely for their revenue on advertising.

Foreign brands are definitely impacting on local brands through competition and takeovers. Some of the greatest competition is in the biggest advertising categories: soap, detergents and soft-drinks. Procter and Gamble, Hindustan Unilever and Colgate Palmolive are competing for the soap and detergents market. Procter and Gamble has made a strategic alliance with Godrej Soaps, the leading Indian maker of soaps and detergents. Coca Cola and Pepsi are fiercely competing for the soft-drink market.

There is a definite visible advertising war between Coca Cola and Pepsi, and billboards in the countryside promote their products at prices cheaper than anywhere else in the world, 5 Rs for 200ml is about 10c. Both companies are increasingly targeting the youth market. Coke made losses in India for many years but was starting to make a profit since the late 1990s. The 1990s have also witnessed increased government spending on advertising and government departments are featured in the client lists of major agencies. The government is advertising in areas such as tourist promotion, army recruitment, aids awareness and is using international agencies in joint ventures. The service sector is another area is also expanding, and with the privatisation of banking and insurance those areas are expected to increase their advertising. After a new code of conduct was issued in the early 1990s, Indian political parties have emerged as a major clients for the advertising sector.

ADVERTISING AGENCIES

The usage of the different advertising media has changed in recent decades, largely due to changes in technology. In the early decades of the 20th Century print was the key medium, as it is today though its influence is declining in relation to television. The impact of media, television, radio, print, outdoor, internet, is influenced by different factors. Literacy and income levels are important for print advertising.

Media usage overall is increasing and the absolute figures for print advertising expenditure are on the increase. Press advertising was 58 per cent of the total in 1999, compared to television at 34 per cent. Print was the major category in 2001 and in 2002, though television is expected to increase its share from 40.7 per cent in 2001 to 41.8 in 2004. Television and print advertising in 2000 accounted for 89 per cent of advertising. There has also been an expansion in magazines for niche markets. Radio accounts for 2.5 per cent of advertising expenditure.

The latest marketing frontier is the internet and Pepsi and Coca Cola are some of the leading marketers in this area. The number of internet users in India is increasing day-by-day and the net users are predominantly male and young. Some of the largest advertisers in India are exploring different strategies and media to attempt to enter the vast rural consumer market, where even a small percentage of market share amounts to millions of consumers. Media alternatives such as video vans and point of purchase video display were an attempt by major advertisers to communicate to rural purchasers in their local language, rather than Hindi and English, the main languages on television.

Many new concepts popped-up and online advertising is one of them. India is pretty new to online advertising but this concept has been around for quiet a long time now. Going by the latest trend you will come to know that new media advertising is the emerging and hottest medium of advertisement.

Now people instead of going for traditional advertising tend to give more weight-age to online advertising. This is mainly due to the fact that it is more targeted maximum exposure. According to various media gurus' online advertising has got a bright future and they also predict that within few years online advertising will experience a boom in India and around the world.

The biggest advantage of online advertising is that many other medium too fall in same bracket and the latest to join the bandwagon is cellular phones. Cellular phones have recently entered into the scope of new media advertising and are predicted to flourish in the coming time. Online advertising's main highlight is that it can be done via various means such as banner ads, pop-up advertisements, and interstitial and even pop-under advertisements.

The biggest advantage of online advertising is that it is relatively cheaper in comparison to other media and can also be done in an attractive manner. Moreover, various small and upcoming businesses can easily go for online advertising. In other words, you can say that it is very attractive in nature and simultaneously entices customers too. Going for online advertising is the wisest choices as it gives the surfer both visual and graphic treat. Also you can use online advertising in any local language and customised message. This means it will be attracting more customers and visitors and ultimately boosting the business. Anyone irrespective of the place he resides can access the Internet from any corner of the globe. However, you will be surprised to know that it has emerged as one of the most convenient ways to promote any brand or company.

MOSTLY ADVERTISED PRODUCTS

The range of products that are advertised reflects the socio-economic profile of the population and disposable income levels. Low cost repeat purchase consumables dominated advertising in India as they do in most emerging economies. The first companies to move into new markets in developing countries tended to be in the areas of low cost repeat purchase consumables: cigarettes, fast food, personal products, cleaning products, soft drinks and pharmaceuticals.

The high level of market concentration in the 1980s, was reflected in the fact that over 50 per cent of market share was accounted for by the three top brands in 17 selected product groups. The changes in the advertising product profile in India in the 1990s reflect changes in the levels of disposable income that occurred in the 1990s for some groups as well as legal changes. Areas of fierce competition in Indian include soft drinks, toothpaste, soaps and detergents.

In 1992, 90 per cent of the most advertised products were repeat purchase consumables with bath soaps and laundry detergents accounting for 45 per cent of the market, and other products included: soft drinks, suitings and textiles, tires, chocolates, cigarettes, tea. The category suitings and textiles, reflected the local custom for people to have their clothes made rather than buying them ready-made but later in the decade this category was no longer a leading product. There was a slight variation in the profile of products advertised on television.

By the mid 1990s the key products in terms of overall advertising spending were: personal care; electronics; cigarette and tobacco; automobiles; pharmaceuticals; food and dairy products; breweries and distilleries with the strongest growth being in the figures for electronics and cigarettes and tobacco. Products most advertised on Doordarshan, included cosmetics, soap and detergents, while the satellite channels in 1997 tended to attract alcohol, consumer durable and expensive clothes advertising. In order of importance in 1999 the key products advertised were: soaps and detergents, household appliances, consumer electronics, food and beverages, cosmetics, pharmaceuticals, services and entertainment. It is interesting that cigarettes and automobiles have slipped off the list of most advertised products. Alcohol was banned from print but allowed in pay television until January 2001. Cigarette and tobacco advertising was permitted in print in the 1990s, were banned in December 2000, but still evident in outdoor advertising.

ADVERTISING STRATEGIES

Advertising in India has been concentrated on the two key media: print and television, with India reflecting the same worldwide trends, with print on the decline and television on the ascendency, and advertising is targeted at the groups that can be reached through those media. Products tend to be advertised to groups that can afford them, or who are future potential purchasers. Advertising strategies vary with the intention of the marketers, especially the international advertisers, their agencies and analyses of the target market.

In the early phases of international entry into the Indian market they targeted the affluent Indians with significant purchasing power and those with disposable income for repeat purchase consumables and increasingly consumer durables. Television advertising was seen to play on the foreign obsessions of many Indians in the early 1990s as well as significantly increasing their desires for advertised products.

Most academic research into advertising strategies seems to have been studies of print advertising, mainly in magazines, which are admittedly easier to document than more ephemeral television advertising, but which are targeted at affluent groups. The National Council for Applied Economic Research has identified the 'very rich and consuming classes' in India as part of an international class with similar lifestyles and consumption habits. This group are educated, travel, own houses, cars, consumer appliances, and in India have servants.

Advertising in certain media, especially magazines, is likely to target this group. A cross cultural comparison of magazine advertising in the US, and India and other countries in the late 1980s saw more visual similarities than differences in advertising practices of advertisements. The magazine profile included *Business India, Reader's Digest, India Today, Femina* and *Woman's Era*. In a comparative content analysis of magazine advertising in India and the US in 2002 Khairullah and Khairullah found the dominant cultural values to be similar and thus made the case for standardisation of advertising, i.e. using advertising in India primarily developed for the American market. The product range of the advertisements was limited to airlines, cars, cigarettes, computers and hotels. These products have been identified as the most likely to be characterised by standardised advertising

Another study by Chandra et.al., which investigated whether American standardised advertising was suitable for the Indian market in 2002, found that market segments were similar to the United States, and that India had a strong middle class with western product experience. They recommended the use of American advertising in India, especially in a diverse market. They did find that durable products were not significantly characterised by standardised advertising any more than non-durable. They were however, cautious in their claims, they did not analyse the media, message or execution and suggested maybe standardised advertising from non-American advertisers might be less suitable for standardisation, which would have to be investigated. They see that one reason companies use standardised advertising is that they view emerging markets as less significant, and used standardised advertising to cut costs.

Advertising campaigns are seen to be getting much more aggressive and focused in recent years which is probably because advertisers are beginning to appreciate the size of the markets and the potential profits to be made in India. There has been considerable increase in market research by key advertisers, with companies like Ogilvie Mather setting up Ogilvy. One marketing agency to help with consumer research, and the establishment of international marketing firms such as MindShare a WPP agency which launched in India in 2001. MindShare was estimated to have cornered 30 percent of the Indian advertising market within a year.

There seems to have been less academic research into the advertising of cheap repeat purchase consumables to the less affluent markets, though there has been considerable market research by key advertisers. Hindustan Unilever Ltd. has been the largest advertiser in India almost every year for decades, and personal products are the biggest category in advertising. As the average income in India is still low, Rs. 2100 per month, a key strategy by large companies like HLL has been to reduce the size of their packages, 'think small', and sell tiny sachets of detergent and shampoo. This makes the product accessible and gets consumers accustomed to using the product.

The advertising industry in India has moved from focusing on demand creation to brand creation and the promotion of specific products. The most successful strategies prior to 1997 were seen to be simple and straightforward messages stressing product benefits. A good example was Rexona deodorant soap sold at Rs 60, compared to other brands selling at Rs150-200, and advertised with a campaign saying that body odour is a problem and Rexona the answer. The market also needs to be ready for the product, for example an American disposable contact lens company spent Rs 30 million in 1996/1997 on advertising but could not sell its product because of its high price according to the Economist Intelligence Unit Limited. Other reasons could be that if people value frugality they may be reluctant to purchase disposable items as an alternative to reusable lenses, or that they have different values about appearance and wearing glasses.

There have been significant changes in recent years and no longer does successful advertising focus only on product benefits, but works through values and value change. By the late 1990s multinational companies were seen to be customising their advertising to the Indian market. Product endorsement by celebrities, and associations with national passions like cricket were other strategies used.

The Korean company LG sponsored the Indian cricket team in the Cricket World Cup in 2003 for example and Adidas, who had previously made their Indian ads in London, started making them in India in 1999, with the advertising agency RKSwamy/BBDO and using an Indian cricket star Sachin Tendulkar. L'Oreal increased its sales dramatically by using the Miss India who became Miss World, Diana Haydin, along with its usual models. In the 1990s the profile of rural consumers was starting to change and greater literacy levels meant brand identification was easier and more product information could be supplied. Previously visual characteristics like colour were seen to be a very important factor in identifying the product for the non-literate, for example the importance of the red colour of Lifebouy packaging from Hindustan Unilever. Lifebouy is India's largest selling soap.

In the 1990s strategies used to tap the vast rural market included using mobile vans with television sets screening Hindi film songs inter-dispersed with product promotions. Ogilvie Outreach, set up to target rural consumers, had expanded its sales force from 2 people to 1,000 people from 1994 to 2000, with another 5,000 working on contract. More recent approaches include games, door to door sales, folk dances, placing of tiles in village wells, putting up shoe racks in temples and sometimes painting the horns of cows and putting up scarecrows. More recent marketing initiatives since 2000 have been precisely targeting rural consumers, who number about 700 million. Activities include setting up e-choupals (cybercafes) in villages and Hindustan Lever's 'Project Shakti', (Shakti means power). Through 'Project Shakti' the company supports rural self-help groups to alleviate poverty and reduce disparities in purchasing power. The groups are provided with a range of its products: Lifebouy Soap, Wheel detergent, A1 tea, Nikhar coconut oil and Clinic Plus Shampoo.

Coca Cola has tried multiple approaches to the Indian market since they returned in 1993, including buying out key local brands Parle and Thums Up. They haven't always been able to get their advertising right, for example in 1997 a television commercial showing a child bungy jumping to get a chocolate bar had to be withdrawn after children died trying to imitate the advertisement. More recently they have Coca Cola has expanded efforts to market to internet users, who number approximately 7 million, ownership being 5.8 million in 2002. They have set up a website (www.enjoyzone.com) with an aim of building an online community with competitions and games. Coca Cola managed to turn around its 2000 Rs.20,000 million loss, by selling smaller bottles in rural markets, this resulted in sales increases of 34 per cent by the beginning of 2002.

The advent of foreign advertisers in India has not always been successful and campaigns that failed in India, which included Nike, Reebok, Johnny Walker, Sony, Panasonic, McDonalds and Coca Cola, caused advertisers to look more closely at their strategies. One of the most dramatically insensitive recent campaigns was that of Cadbury-Schweppes which compared its chocolate to Kashmir: 'Too tempting. Too good to share', which caused a major outrage and had to be withdrawn.

REGULATIONS AND CENSORSHIP

India's constitution, set up at the time of independence in 1947, has a provision for freedom of speech and expression, though commercial advertising was excluded from this provision in a Supreme Court Ruling in 1960. A number of laws helped define the limitations of advertising. In 1969 the Monopolies and Restrictive Trade Practices Act included misleading advertising in the definition of 'unfair trade practices', including misrepresentation regarding price, quality and also prohibited the practice 'bait and switches'.

In 1954 the Drugs and Magic Remedies Act restricted advertising of some contraceptive devices or those that would facilitate miscarriages, along with the banning of false claims from drugs and medication. The Indecent Representation of Women Act in 1986 endeavoured to restrict exploitation of women by the media and was a response to consumer demands. Other acts restrict the use of certain emblems and names; the conduct of promotions and competitions for prizes; comparative advertising that involves defamation, and financial advertising claims. There are also ethical codes of conduct established by the Advertising Standards Council of India and the India Newspaper Society.

A new code of conduct issued in 1990 has led to Indian politics emerging as a major client for the advertising sector. Unsubstantiated claims also do not get past the Advertising Standards Council, such as the rejection of Hutchison Max's claim to be 'the best cellular service in India' which would be acceptable in other countries. In 1993 the government lifted its ban on foreign advertising on 5 of Doordarshan's 5 satellite channels, but still kept the ban on Channel 1, and still banned the advertising of alcohol (4th October, 1993). Before 1994, the national television network banned the advertising of foreign goods and services but in 1994 Doordarshan, lifted its ban on the advertising of foreign products such banks and financial services and certain other products such as matrimonial agencies and hair dyes. In April 2001, the new female Minister of Information and Broadcasting, had a number of advertisements taken off the national broadcaster Doordarshan for being 'distasteful' and 'degrading for women'. Kissing was also banned from television. The key products that are banned in broadcast media are alcohol, cigarettes and tobacco.

SCOPE OF ADVERTISING

The whole purpose of advertising is to sell products or ideas, so the massive expansion of foreign companies and advertising, whether coming from overseas or created in India, has meant the massive expansion of the sales of foreign products. The liberalisation of the Indian economy has led to the accelerated entry of foreign business and foreign advertising agencies to sell the products of foreign products to the vast potential Indian market of over a billion people.

Though there are approximately about 25 per cent living at or below the poverty line, the expanding potential markets represented by those above the poverty line number hundreds of millions for low priced repeat purchase consumer goods, and many millions for those able to purchase consumer durables and luxury goods. Advertisers are using considerable ingenuity to develop strategies to enter these markets.

The increases in advertising expenditure and the promotion of foreign products have impacts on culture, through the undermining of traditional habits and behaviours, the creation of new wants and desires, often for products like softdrinks that have no nutritional benefit, and also by strategies that rework cultural values and beliefs. The roles of men, women and children are changing, traditional places within home and family, concepts of beauty, identity and personal cleanliness are undergoing major change. The overall impact of massive increases of foreign company advertising is the acceleration of India into the culture and ideology of consumerism, the expansion of foreign businesses into India and the export of profits to foreign corporations.

Advertising professionals in India have to be fully aware of the challenge and responsibility trust on them by virtue of a vast unexploited potential, on the one hand, and the resistance they encounter from various quarters on the other. This requires their looking beyond their own narrow areas of operation. A great deal of co-operative endeavour is required in order to put advertising on a sound footing. This has to be backed by research, the back of which is a major draw back for advertising decisions.

There has to be a greater willingness on the part of all persons and actions concerned with advertising to innovate and experiment. This calls for an unconventional approach, as applicable, whether it is towards idea, content of the message, creative strategy or evaluation of tenses. Stereotyping is the curse of advertising is a real danger against which the industry has to guard itself. This may be seen for instance in heavy reliance on the standard mass media, or in creative execution. A advertisement for textiles products for instance, look alike. This type of situation may render all such advertising ineffective. It is, basically, in the interest of advertisers to get a proper payoff from their investment in sing agencies, too, can justify their existence only if advertising products result.

The quality of advertising and its social acceptance are the two sides of the coin. Advertising has to reflect social norms, value and aspirations, it will be irrelevant and wasteful. Nevertheless, various problems arise hence the need for legislation and self regulation has been felt wide. This subject should be treated with urgency it requires. The sensible and practicable guidelines can be developed and an institutional frame work established for self regulation, the greater will be the benefit for the advertising industry. Imposition of such discipline from win be preferable to legislation. Self regulation can be more effective, because of its expediency, as against lengthy legal processes. Moreover, be provide much need flexibility. If recent trends towards increasing professionalisation are any guide, there are grounds to believe that the advertising industry will be able to evolve norms of conduct for itself which will enable it to continue growing and making its due contribution to person and the nation.

BIBLIOGRAPHY

Agnew, Clark M. and Neil O'Brien, *Television Advertising,* New York, McGraw-Hill, 1958.

Bhatia, Tej K., *Advertising in Rural India: Language, Marketing Communication, and Consumerism.* Institute for the Study of Languages and Cultures of Asia and Africa. Tokyo University of Foreign Studies. Tokyo Press: Japan. 2000.

Campbell, Richard, *Media and Culture: An Introduction to Mass Communication,* New York: St. Martin's Press, 1998.

Cook, Guy, *The Discourse of Advertising,* London: Routledge, 2nd edition, 2001.

David Ogilvy and Sir Alan Parker, *Confessions of an Advertising Man,* Southbank Publishing, 2004.

Gary Dahl, *Advertising For Dummies,* For Dummies, 2007.

Gavin Lucas and Michael Dorrian, *Guerrilla Advertising: Unconventional Brand Communication,* Laurence King Publishers, 2006.

Geis, Michael L., *The Language of Television Advertising,* New York: Academic Press, 1982.

Graydon, Shari *Made You Look—How Advertising Works and Why You Should Know,* Toronto: Annick Press, 2003.

Heighton, Elizabeth J., *Advertising in the Broadcast and Cable Media,* 2nd ed. Belmont, Calif.: Wadsworth Pub. Co., 1984.

Hettinger, Herman S., *A Decade of Radio Advertising,* Chicago: The University of Chicago Press, 1933.

Howard, Herbert H. and Michael S. Kievman, with the assistance of Darrel Holt, Kent Sidel, Mark Banks, *Radio and TV Programming,* Columbus, Ohio: Grid Pub., 1983.

Joe Plummer, Steve Rappaport, Taddy Hall, and Robert Barocci, *The Online Advertising Playbook: Proven Strategies and Tested Tactics from the Advertising Research Foundation*, Wiley, 2007

John Caples and Fred E. Hahn, *Tested Advertising Methods*, Prentice Hall Business Classics, 1998.

Klein, Naomi. *No Logo: Taking Aim at the Brand Bullies*. New York: Picador, 2000.

Laermer, Richard; Simmons, Mark, *Punk Marketing*, New York : Harper Collins, 2007.

Lockhart, Ron and Dick Weissman, *Audio in Advertising: A Practical Guide to Producing and Recording Music, Voiceovers, and Sound Effects*, New York : F. Unger Pub. Co., 1982.

Mario Pricken, *Creative Advertising*, Thames & Hudson; 2 edition , 2008.

Petley, Julian, "Advertising". North Mankato, Minnesota: Smart Apple Media, 2002.

Sandra Moriarty, Nancy Mitchell, and William D. Wells, *Advertising: Principles and Practice*, Prentice Hall, 8th edition, 2008.

Young, Charles E., *The Advertising Handbook*, Ideas in Flight, Seattle, WA, 2005.

More titles are available in

MANAGEMENT BOOKS

1.	Art of Advertising **(New)**	125/-
2.	Art of Marketing **(New)**	125/
3.	Art of Growing Business **(New)**	125/-
4.	Art of Retailing **(New)**	125/-
5.	Art of Leadership **(New)**	125/-
6.	Art of Team Building **(New)**	125/-
7.	Art of Corporate Communication **(New)**	125/-
8.	Art of Organisational Management **(New)**	125/-
9.	How to Negotiate Effectively? **(New)**	150/-
10.	Improve your Marketing and Grow your Business **(New)**	150/-
11.	What Customers Really Want **(New)**	150/-
12.	Effective Presentation **(New)**	150/-
13.	The Right Decision Every Time **(New)**	150/-
14.	Develop Your Decision Making Skills	95/-

15.	Develop Your Team Building Skills	95/-
16.	Develop Your Skills to Conduct Effective Meetings	95/-
17.	How to Export Import	95/-
18.	How to Use Money	95/-
19.	How to Start My Business	95/-
20.	How to Organise My Office	95/-
21.	How to Manufacture My Products	95/-
22.	How to Promote & Advertise	95/-
23.	How to Sell My Products	95/-
24.	How to Develop & Maintain Quality	95/-

Lotus

PRESS

(Publishers & Distributors)

4263/3, Ansari Road, Darya Ganj, New Delhi- 110002
Ph.: 32903912, 23280047, 9811594448
E-mail: lotus_press@sify.com
www.lotuspress.co.in